RECOVERING

from the

LOSSES

OF LIFE

H. NORMAN WRIGHT

with Learning Activities by Kay Moore

Lifeway Press
Nashville, Tennessee

ACKNOWLEDGEMENTS

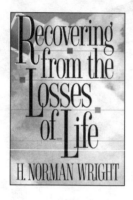

Recovering from the Losses of Life was originally published by Fleming H. Revell and is available in its original version in Christian bookstores. We want to thank Baker Book House for making this book available to the LifeWay Press for its use.

Recovering from the Losses of Life, LIFE® Support Group Series Edition
Copyright © 1995 by Fleming H. Revell

For help for facilitators and leaders in carrying out LIFE® Support Group Series ministries in your church, call 1-615-251-5613.

Item 7200-27   ISBN 0-8054-9874-5   Dewey Decimal Number 155.2
Subject Heading: JOY//SORROW

Unless otherwise indicated, biblical quotations are from the Holy Bible, *New International Version*, copyright © 1973, 1978, 1984 by International Bible Society (NIV). Other versions used: *New American Standard Bible*. (NASB) © The Lockman Foundation, 1960, 1962, 1963, 1968, 1971, 1972, 1973, 1975, 1977; *The Holy Bible, New King James Version* (NKJV), copyright © 1982 by Thomas Nelson, Inc.; *The Living Bible* (TLB), paraphrased , © 1971 Tyndale House Publishers; the *King James Version* (KJV). Used by permission.

Printed in the United States of America

Table of Contents

THE AUTHORS

 H. Norman Wright is the founder and director of Christian Marriage Enrichment and is in private practice at Family Counseling and Enrichment in Tustin, California. He is the author of more than 50 books, including *Communication: Key to Your Marriage, Quiet Times for Couples, Always Daddy's Girl,* and with his wife Joyce, *I'll Love You Forever.*

 Kay W. Moore is a writer, editor, and speaker on family and relationship issues. She has been Design Editor for the LIFE_® Support Group Series, is the author of several books on family life, and has led numerous support groups. She wrote the learning activities for *Recovering from the Losses of Life* LIFE_® Support Group Series Edition and wrote the facilitator's guide.

LIFE_® Support Group Series Editorial Team
Betty Hassler, Design Editor
Dale McCleskey, Editor
Kenny Adams, Manuscript Assistant

David Walley, Team Leader/LIFE_® Support Group Series Specialist

Graphics by Lori Putnam
Cover Design by Edward Crawford

On the Road to Recovery

Case in point

> ## WITHDRAWN AND ANGRY
>
> Edith's son Marty died in a boating accident. Two years after the accident Edith is still withdrawn and angry about everything that occurred. Just after the tragedy happened, Edith's friends rallied around her and tried to get her to go places with them to help her get her mind off of things. Edith refused to go with them and said she preferred to stay at home. She kept Marty's room just at it looked when he lived there and refused to sort through his clothes even after two years passed. After a while Edith's friends got tired of asking her out, only to be rejected, so they stopped contacting her. Edith also dropped out of church because of her anger at God for not sparing Marty. She believes she has no use for a group for bereaved people at her church. She lives the life of a recluse except for the time she spends at work each day.
>
> When people ask Edith how she is doing in the aftermath of the tragedy, her standard comment is, "I'm doing just fine. Just fine." But Edith fools no one when she keeps up this kind of false front. Inside she feels defeated and hopeless. She believes that her faith is worthless in the wake of this tragic incident. Many times she feels close to giving up on life.

Many of us can identify with Edith because of the hopelessness and despair that we have felt about the loss we have sustained. Edith experienced grief because of the death of a loved one, but many of us have experienced the same kind of devastation because of some other loss—the loss of a job, loss of a location because of a move, loss of health and mobility, loss of a dream or goal, loss of children in the home because of their graduation or marriage, loss of a pet, loss of a friendship or long-time dating relationship, loss of a spouse through divorce, or loss of a limb, to name a few. Because—like Edith—we allow these events to thoroughly undo us, we can have harmful reactions that can cause us to sustain much emotional, spiritual, and even physical destruction.

If Edith continues on her present course, she will cut herself off from the fellowship of all those who try to help her. She will not take advantage of the hope and healing that can occur by depending on God as her source of strength. Her depression could affect her physically if she refuses to seek healthy outlets for her stress. Her reaction even could affect her employment if her downtrodden attitude about life keeps her from doing her best at work.

Course goal

Recovering from the Losses of Life LIFE® Support Group Series Edition would help Edith take some positive steps toward recovering from her loss. It would help her realize that rather than being buffeted by this unwelcome event in her life, she has the power, through Christ, to make decisions that will determine how her loss will affect her future.

She can learn to take certain steps that can move her toward healing. In a group with others who have undergone similar losses, she can begin to understand that she is not alone in her feelings of isolation and helplessness.

In Recovering from the Losses of Life LIFE® Support Group Series Edition you will study to change present behavior. You will learn—

What's in it for you

- how to acknowledge and talk about your losses to help you face the future in a more Christ-honoring way;
- how to identify secondary losses that result from your initial loss;
- how to recognize the feelings of depression, anxiety, hurt, and anger that loss generates and how to deal with these effectively;
- various types of unresolved grief that can disturb the normal recovery process;
- how changing your relationship to the person or thing you lost will speed your healing;
- how to decide to do something constructive with your loss.

For example, instead of withdrawing from life, Edith can recognize that she needs to face her losses more squarely and talk about them rather than covering up the fact that she is hurting by saying everything is fine. She can realize some secondary losses she has suffered, such as the loss of identity as a mother and loss of her future dreams for Marty. She can learn to identify the anger, depression, hurt, and other feelings that surround her and learn positive ways to express these emotions rather than pretending they do not exist. She can learn how her withdrawing and her refusing to make certain decisions about her future is disturbing the normal recovery process. She can learn some positive ways to keep Marty's memory alive instead of preserving his room as some kind of unhealthy shrine. She can learn to be patient with herself, since the process of recovery is an ongoing one which involves learning coping skills instead of reaching some magic point in which the hurting totally stops. And she can be reminded of God's faithfulness and presence in the midst of suffering.

On the inside back cover you will find an illustration that we call the course map. This course map will help you visualize where you are going on this journey.

How this course fits in

Recovering from the Losses of Life LIFE® Support Group Series Edition is part of the LIFE® Support Group Series, an educational system of discovery-group and support-group resources for providing Christian ministry and emotional support to individuals in areas of social, emotional, and physical need. These resources deal with such life issues as chemical dependency, codependency, abuse recovery, eating disorders, low self-worth, painful pasts, and divorce. Individuals using LIFE® Support Group Series courses will be led through recovery to discipleship and ministry.

Recovering from the Losses of Life LIFE® Support Group Series Edition is a support-group course designed to be basic to any church's support-group ministry. A support-group studies dysfunctional family issues and other sensitive emotional issues that individuals face. A carefully selected group facilitator guides discussion of the topics and helps group members process what they have learned during their study. The group is not a therapy group. Rather, this is a self-help group, in which group members help each other by talking in a safe, loving environment. An important part of healing from loss involves being around people who accept you as you are and who let you be at whatever stage of grieving you find yourself. It provides a setting in which you can share without restraint with other people undergoing similar losses.

How to study the book

Recovering from the Losses of Life LIFE® Support Group Series Edition is an integrated course of study. To achieve the full benefit, prepare your individual assignments and participate in the group sessions.

To achieve the greatest benefit from this course, ask your church to schedule this course for the full nine sessions that this workbook includes. However, for churches that believe they can offer only an abbreviated schedule to accommodate the often-pressured life situations of people experiencing loss, the first six sessions represent the core sessions in Recovering from the Losses of Life LIFE® Support Group Series Edition, and the last three sessions are optional. Your church may add any of all of the last three that time will allow.

Study Tips. Five days a week (which compose a unit) you will be expected to study a segment of content material. You may need from 30 to 60 minutes of study time each day. Even if you find that you can study the material in less time, spread out the study over five days. This will give you more time to apply the truths to your life. Study at your own pace. Study the material as if H. Norman Wright is sitting at your side helping you learn. When the book asks you a question or gives you an assignment, respond immediately. Each assignment is indented and appears in boldface type. When we ask you to respond in writing, a pencil appears beside the assignment. For example, an assignment will look like the one that follows:

 Read Psalm 139:13. Write what the verse tells about God's care for you.

In an actual activity, a line would appear below each assignment. You would write your answer on this line. When we ask you to respond in a nonwritten manner—for example, by thinking or praying about a matter— an ¶ appears beside the assignment. This type of assignment will look like this:

Stop and pray. Thank God for being with you during the painful times.

Getting the most from the course

In most cases your "personal tutor" will give you some feedback about your response—for example, you may see a suggestion about what you might have written. This process is designed to help you learn the material and apply the concepts more effectively. Do not deny yourself valuable learning by skipping the learning activities.

Set a definite time and select a quiet place where you can study with little interruption. Keep a Bible handy for times when the material asks you to look up Scripture. Memorizing Scripture is an important part of your work. Set aside a portion of your study period for memory work. Make notes of problems, questions, or concerns that arise as you study. You will discuss many of these during your support-group sessions. Write these matters in the margin of this textbook so you can find them easily.

Support-Group Session. Once each week, attend a Recovering from the Losses of Life support group session. A group session is designed to help you discuss the content you studied the previous week and to share personal responses to issues and problems. These groups provide a safe and loving environment for personal and spiritual healing, growth, and recovery.

The support group adds a needed dimension to your learning. If you are not involved in a group study, try to enlist some friends or associates who have experienced or are experiencing loss and who will work through this course with you.

Approach your church leaders about beginning such a group. Recovering from the Losses of Life LIFE® Support Group Series Edition Facilitator's Guide provides guidance and learning activities for these sessions. (For orders or inquiries call the Customer Service Center, 1-800-458-2772. Ask for item 7200-25.)

A key decision

Recovering from the Losses of Life LIFE® Support Group Series Edition is written with the assumption that you already have received Jesus Christ as your Savior and that you have Him guiding you in the healing process. If you have not yet made the crucial decision to receive Christ, you will find in unit 2 guidance for how to do so. You will benefit more from Recovering from the Losses of Life LIFE® Support Group Series Edition if you have Jesus working in and guiding your life. Many people can testify that in the aftermath of a loss they have found Jesus to be their friend. Allow Jesus to work in your life during this time of recovery.

People who are in loss situations can know that what happened to them isn't as important as is how they react to it. How they react will determine their ability to recover. Recovering from the Losses of Life LIFE® Support Group Series Edition provides some suggestions for healthy ways to react that can lay the groundwork for their healing. May healing begin in your life as God guides your work in this book.

Editor's note:

Because of the church program need for short-term groups, Recovering from the Losses of Life LIFE® Support Group Series Edition is designed for group study in from six to nine weeks. While units one through six make up the core content of this book, unit seven contains key biblical content. The unit will help you to see your loss from God's perspective. If you choose to use the shorter plan and study only the first six units, we encourage you also to make plans either as a group or individually to work through unit seven.

The Losses of Life

Case in point

SEPARATING THE LOSSES

Cynthia told her group, "When my only child married, he and his new wife moved half a continent away to live. When they left the church for their honeymoon, we didn't see them again for six months. I was so excited about the wedding that I didn't realize how much I would miss my son.

"I continued to put on a good front and denied that I was experiencing loss in the midst of this excitement. Now I realize that I refused to deal with my grief about the loss of my son."

What did Cynthia need to do in order to move on with her life and to react to these events in a Christ-honoring way? In this unit you will learn more about the grief process.

What you'll learn

This week you will
- discover that identifying and talking about your losses can help you face the future in a more Christ-honoring way;
- learn that ungrieved childhood losses can prevent you from recovering from adult losses;
- identify the effects that previous losses—effects that were not obvious to you at the time—had on you;
- describe how the frequency and finality of losses can contribute to the feeling of despair;
- learn how the fear of loss affects you and how to see your losses in the context of life experiences.

What you'll study

Loss: A Constant Companion	Some Ways We Cope	Not-So-Obvious Losses	Frequency, Finality of Loss	Threatened Losses
DAY 1	DAY 2	DAY 3	DAY 4	DAY 5

Memory verse

This week's verse of Scripture to memorize
Trust in the Lord with all your heart, and lean not on your own understanding; in all your ways acknowledge Him and He shall direct your paths.
—Proverbs 3:5-6, NKJV

Loss: A Constant Companion

Today's Objective:
You will discover that identifying and talking about your losses can help you face the future in a more Christ-honoring way.

The woman standing in front of the large group radiated confidence and assurance. As she interacted with the people, she smiled and laughed. She obviously was in good spirits. Life seemed to be going well for her, but several of the people in the group she led appeared to be in just the opposite state of mind. An air of sadness hung over them. A few of them sat stoically. They did not smile or laugh, nor did they seem confident or assured. After a while, the speaker noticed these individuals who seemed to be struggling. She asked to speak with them during the break. "I couldn't help noticing that several of you appear sad and are struggling with some problems this evening," she said. "Could you tell me what your concerns are?"

One by one, the stories poured out. One man had lost his job after 27 years. One woman's son was in the last stages of AIDS. Another woman's husband had died three months previously. And one man had chronic, undiagnosed back pains.

 You too may be struggling with a serious concern—a concern that has brought you to this group. Below describe the issue which prompted you to seek support in recovering from life's losses.

_____

_____

The speaker at the group meeting listened attentively to the stories of recent upsets. Then she said: "I can see we all have something in common. We're all dealing with significant losses, and we're experiencing a lot of pain."

A man in the group spoke up. "It's true that we are, but you couldn't be struggling with a major loss. We've watched you this evening, and you are nowhere near where any of us are. You're not struggling as we are."

"I was where you are… and it was difficult."

"You're right," the speaker replied, "when you say that I'm not struggling as you are. I'm not now—but I was, and it was difficult. Two years ago, I was in the same type of situation as many of you are: an unfaithful husband, divorce, loss of a home, and my dad died suddenly of a heart attack. I was deep in despair. I still grieve. I am still recovering from my losses. I'm just at a different phase of the grief process. I was where you are, and someday you will be where I am."

 As it applies to your loss, how do you feel about the statement "someday you will be where I am"?

❏ Nothing will ever change for me. I feel as though I'll always feel as much despair as I do now.
❏ I want to be farther along in the grieving process, but I seem to be only able to take small steps, with lots of setbacks.
❏ I believe that with God's help and the support of others, I can arrive at the point where I struggle less with my loss.

❏ Other _____

In this exercise you may have checked one statement that seems to apply to you most of the time, or you may have had difficulty checking just one because you believe that all three statements describe you at one time or another. You may want to be farther along and believe God and others can help you, but you struggle with peaks and valleys in the grief process.

A silent conspiracy

Loss is a simple, four-letter word that is one of our constant companions throughout life, but we don't talk about it very often. Like a silent conspiracy, we seem to have an unspoken agreement with others not to talk about our losses.

Nobody likes to lose. Life is supposed to be filled with winners. Look at the headlines on the sports page. Winners, not losers, receive the praises. Losing hurts. A small loss or a large one—it doesn't matter. It hurts. And it hurts even more because no one has taught us to expect or how to deal with the losses of life. We want to be winners. We want success. We want to be in control of our lives, so we build walls around ourselves with signs that say, "Losses—No Trespassing!" Then, when losses occur, we feel violated.

Too often, we tend to blame the loss on the person who is suffering it. We make comments like—

- "She must not have been a good wife if he left her."
- "They failed as parents. Otherwise that child would have stayed in church and wouldn't have become involved with the wrong crowd."
- "He lost his job. I wonder what he did wrong."
- "If they had been living the Christian life, this wouldn't have happened."

 Have you ever had any of the thoughts just listed about another person or about yourself? In the list above, put a check in the margin by any remark that you remember thinking or saying about yourself or others, or write below any similar statements that you may have thought or said.

_____

_____

And as He passed by, He saw a man blind from birth. And His disciples asked Him, saying, "Rabbi, who sinned, this man or his parents, that he should be born blind?" Jesus answered, "It was neither that this man sinned, nor his parents; but it was in order that the works of God might be displayed in him."

–John 9:1-3, NASB

That type of attitude has been with us for a long time. In John 9:1-3, which appears in the margin, the disciples expressed such thoughts to Jesus about a blind man.

Attitudes of blame, either toward ourselves or others, do not help us learn to properly grieve the losses of life. In this study you'll learn how to set these attitudes aside and to develop Christ-honoring ways of dealing with and moving beyond your losses.

 When we hurt, we often have difficulty praying. Below write a few words you want to say to God. Do not worry about complete sentences or complete thoughts. Just write words or phrases that express your feelings, thoughts, or needs.

_____

_____

Some Ways We Cope

Today's Objective:
You will learn that ungrieved
childhood losses can prevent
you from recovering from adult
losses.

You may be participating in this study because of a major loss you have sustained recently, but you actually have already experienced many losses in your life. At the time, you may not have realized that what you experienced—like graduating from high school and leaving friends—actually were losses. How you respond and what you let losses do to you will affect the rest of your life.

You can't avoid loss or shrug it off. Loss is not the enemy; not facing its existence is. Unfortunately, many of us have been more skilled in denying loss than we are in facing and accepting the losses of life.

✎ **Below describe a loss in your life that you didn't identify as a loss at the time it happened.**

_____

_____

Cynthia responded: "When my only child married, he and his new wife moved half a continent away to live. When they left the church for their honeymoon, we didn't see them again for six months. I was so excited about the wedding that I didn't realize how much I would miss my son. I continued to put on a good front and denied that I was experiencing loss in the midst of this excitement. Now I realize that I refused to deal with my grief about the loss of my son."

Even if you attempt to ignore the loss, the emotional experience of it is implanted in your heart and mind, and no eraser will remove it. When you have any kind of attachment, you cannot avoid a loss when the tie is broken. Life is full of relationships with people, things, and dreams that break up. As each change takes place, you either identify and experience the grief that accompanies the change, or you refuse to grieve the loss.

You either identify and experience the grief, or you refuse to grieve the loss.

Children who experience too many losses have more difficulty dealing with their future adolescent and adult losses. Children do not have the coping skills and defense mechanisms that adults have. They don't possess the verbal skills to generate alternatives the way adults can.

Many adults experienced as children some form of loss that created an over-sensitivity to similar reactions and responses as adults. One 40-year-old man told this story about when he was growing up: Whenever he was noisy or disruptive, his parents withheld affection as a way to punish and control him. He felt empty and hurt each time he experienced this loss of love. This affected him so deeply that when his friends visited him, he felt embarrassed if they were loud or noisy in front of his parents. Today, he still is highly sensitive to the responses of others in noisy situations, even when he isn't responsible for the noise.

Unfortunately, most adults are unable to help their children grieve because they themselves never learned to grieve effectively. When a child doesn't grieve over a loss, a similar loss in adult life can reactivate the feelings associated with the childhood experience. Thus a childhood loss can predispose us to oversensitivity and depression.

After living in the same town for 15 years, Janet and her husband moved to a new city. In their former town, this husband and wife were deeply involved in their church and had many friends. They had reared their children there and had celebrated each Christmas with the same close friends, but when they moved, they left all of that behind.

Janet's husband started his new job immediately, but Janet had to start over and rebuild from scratch. For the first two years, she was depressed and couldn't understand why.

Janet's childhood loss

Through counseling Janet finally recognized the reason for depression. As a child she felt very close to her grandmother, but then her grandmother died suddenly. Within weeks, her family moved from town to the country, where the nearest neighbor was a mile away. As she and her counselor talked and the connection became clear, she then was able to grieve as she never had about her grandmother and that childhood move. In time, her depression lifted.

✎ **Can you identify a loss in your life that you've never fully grieved? Below describe this loss.**

_____

_____

How do you believe this ungrieved loss affects you today?

_____

_____

When we do not grieve our childhood losses, we "compound" our losses. We begin to pile one loss on top of another. Instead of experiencing one loss at a time and focusing the grief on that loss, compounding creates a bigger loss. Each loss appears to be larger than it actually is.

We need to isolate each loss, see it for what it is, respond to it, and then deal with the other losses one at a time. When we don't grieve effectively, unresolved reactions and feelings lead to a higher level of discomfort, and these unresolved issues continue to keep us from experiencing life to the fullest. In unit 2 we'll explore this topic in more detail.

You may find you need extended study about this area of ungrieved childhood losses. Another support-group resource, *Making Peace with Your Past*, and its sequel, *Moving Beyond Your Past*, both by Tim Sledge (Nashville: LifeWay Press) can provide further information about how to grieve—and recover from—childhood losses.

🕊 **Thinking about ungrieved childhood losses can be a painful experience but can help you greatly in the long run. Ask God to continue to give you the courage you need to look at difficult losses. Ask Him to help you trust Him in the healing process.**

Begin to memorize this week's Scripture passage, Proverbs 3:5-6 (look back at page 9 to refresh your memory). Write the passage three times in the margin.

DAY 3

Today's Objective:
You will examine the effect previous losses—effects that did not seem obvious to you at the time—had on you.

Not-So-Obvious Losses

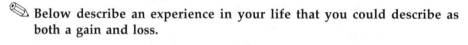

Life is a blending of loss and gain. In creation, loss is the ingredient of growth. A bud is lost when it turns into a beautiful rose. A seed must be lost before a plant can push its way up through the soil.

Graduating from high school produced a loss of status, friends, and familiarity, but most of us looked forward to it, for it meant going on with our lives. When we are young, we celebrate some of our losses as much as we mourn them. Most of these early losses are developmental and necessary. We can accept them fairly easily. But often we focus on the gain without remembering that some loss usually is attached to it. Change involves some form of loss of the way things used to be.

Below describe an experience in your life that you could describe as both a gain and loss.

_____

_____

We feel as a loss any event that threatens our understanding of the meaning of life. Our beliefs and expectations come under attack. The phrase, "How could that person have done such a thing?" expresses this confusion. Sometimes a person we hold in high esteem disappoints us. An admired public official is exposed for moral wrongdoing. A coach or a teacher teaches by one set of rules but lives by another. A friend lets us down in a big way.

Below describe an experience in which someone disappointed you.

_____

_____

More and more immigrants are moving to our country. These immigrants experience a major cultural loss of lifestyle. Gone are the normal and familiar elements, such as road signs, money, language, food, familiar faces, role patterns, and relationships that give life meaning. Missionaries who move to new fields to serve face major adjustments and losses. Periodically they return to their homeland to encounter new losses as they confront the rapid changes of our economy, values, and lifestyle. Economic losses abound today.

The following five paragraphs describe many kinds of losses. As you read the paragraphs underline at least three not-so-obvious losses you have experienced in the past. Circle at least three losses you are experiencing now.

Loss of face

Other, more subtle losses affect us. We may be aware of the pain of an experience, but we don't identify it as a loss. A minor failure or "putting your foot in your mouth" socially can create embarrassment, shame, or disappointment. The expression "loss of face" recognizes that these experiences are losses.

Losses can be obvious: a loved one dies, someone steals your car, someone vandalizes your house. Other losses may not be so obvious: changing jobs, receiving a B instead of an A, getting less than you had hoped for in a raise, moving, illness (loss of health), a new teacher, the change from an office with windows to one without, success or achievement—the loss of a challenge or of relationships with fellow workers, a son or daughter going off to school, the loss of an ideal, a dream, or a lifelong goal. All of these are losses, but because they may not be easy to recognize, we do not identify them as such. Therefore, we do not spend time and energy dealing with them.

Many of the losses in life are related to aging. As we grow older, the dreams and beliefs of childhood begin to crumble and change. Remember the first time you had a crush on a member of the opposite sex? Childhood and adolescent romances are filled with losses—some daily, even hourly! Moving on from school to school, failing a grade, dropping out, leaving home for college, or just moving out all involve an element of loss—even if you planned for the change.

An element of loss

When you hit the job market, losses multiply with rejections. Someone else gets the raise or promotion, deals fall through, court cases are lost, businesses fail, the economy falters, you get stuck in a "going nowhere" job.

Then we experience physical losses. We lose our youth, our beauty, our smooth skin, our muscle tone, our shape, our hair, our vision and hearing, our mobility, and our independence. As we age, the losses take on a different flavor. Now they seem to be more frequent, permanent, and in many cases, negative. Who rejoices over losing hair, teeth, or graduating to bifocals or even trifocals? Sometimes these losses seem to build on other losses.

✎ **Were you able to identify three losses of each type?** ❑ **Yes** ❑ **No**

As you reflect on some of these not-so-obvious losses, you may react by thinking, "Yes, it's true. I experienced (or, am experiencing) that loss, but it was no big deal." But are you being honest with yourself?

Recognizing losses for what they are and not trying to skim over them but honestly acknowledging their effect on you can help you learn to react in a healthy way when you experience obvious, major losses.

❦ **Stop and pray. Ask God to help you look at life's losses in a new way. Thank Him for helping you through some of these tough times in the past even though at the time you may not have identified these situations as losses.**

✎ **Below write your own paraphrase of Proverbs 3:5-6, this week's Scripture memory verse.**

_____

_____

Trust in the Lord with all your heart, and lean not on your own understanding; in all your ways acknowledge Him and He shall direct your paths.
—Proverbs 3:5-6, NKJV

Frequency, Finality of Loss

Today's Objective:
You will describe how the frequency and finality of losses can contribute to the despair you feel.

Consider also the frequency of losses. Early in our lives, we don't usually lose many of our friends through death. But in our later years, the deaths of friends become much more frequent. The longer we live, the more losses of friends and relatives we experience.

When you are younger, you may have one physical problem, and you corrected it. But now, these problems accumulate. Muscles don't work as well or recover as fast. You're slower in your response time. One day you notice that, besides the new glasses, people are talking in softer tones, and you even have to increase the television volume!

We seem to deal with losses best when they are infrequent. But after mid-life we move into a time zone of accumulating losses. We have difficulty dealing with the next loss when we still are recovering from the present one. Our coping skills may be overtaxed. If we never developed grieving skills, these losses will be quite a jolt to us.

✎ **Can you think of a time in which the frequency of losses itself posed a difficulty for you? Below describe this time.**

_____

_____

_____

Heightened sense of loss

One man answered this way: "All in the same year my daughter graduated from high school and went away to college, and I moved to a new job in a new city. None of these were sad events, and yet because they all happened at the same time, this heightened my sense of loss."

The other difficulty with losses is their finality. If at age 27 you lose a job, you simply look for another. But what if at age 57 you lose your job of 30 years? What do you do now, especially if this is all you know how to do, and your skills aren't in demand anymore? Losing a spouse when you are older is limiting as well. If you divorce or your partner dies when you are young, you more easily can find another mate. As you get older, the prospect of remarriage becomes more difficult.

✎ **Is age a factor in your loss that is contributing to the despair you feel? If so, describe your situation.**

_____

_____

_____

In his book *Losses in Later Life*, R. Scott Sullender shows how handicapped people can teach us to turn life's losses into triumphs.

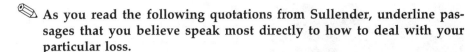 **As you read the following quotations from Sullender, underline passages that you believe speak most directly to how to deal with your particular loss.**

"There is a handicapped person in your future: you! Handicapped persons are dealing in the present moment with what you and I will have to deal with later. Sooner or later each of us will have to deal with one or several major losses in our health. Then we will travel down the same path that the handicapped person currently walks. Then we will know their pain, frustration, and sufferings. Perhaps if we could learn from them now, whatever our age, we would be better prepared for our own future."

Sullender says that handicapped people demonstrate that the things that make people truly spirit filled are not physical qualities but are the attributes that Paul mentioned in Galatians 5:22-23 and those that Jesus mentioned in Matthew 5:3-10. He noted that neither of these passages mentioned physical beauty or even physical health.

Sullender went on to say:

"Handicapped persons also can teach us how to suffer and how to rise above bodily limitations. Sometimes pain cannot be fixed, nor can all limitations be conquered. Most of us will have to deal with pain and limitations, at first in minor ways and later in major ways. We will learn new meanings for the word 'courage.' Either we will rise above our limitations and learn to live with them or we shall sink to new lows of despair, bitterness and helplessness. The choice depends largely on the strength of our courage.

"In a sense, then, a handicap or a loss of health can become a gift. It never starts out that way. Initially it is a horrible loss. If through the loss, however, we can learn to nurture our spiritual qualities and learn the art of suffering, well then we will have transformed our loss into a gain. We will have grown through our loss. We will have risen above our loss precisely by not letting it defeat us, but by letting it propel us forward into a more advanced stage of human existence. Admittedly, not everyone makes such a major leap forward. Neither have some human beings made it past a Sunday school theology. Yet the loss of health in later life, as horrible as it seems, can be the opportunity for growing toward an even greater level of spiritual maturity."[1]

In the last paragraph, Sullender referred to loss as leading to a possible opportunity of growth. In what ways can you see that this might be possible in your life?

_____

_____

Below write a prayer, asking God to show you how He intends for your loss to help you become more spiritually mature.

_____

_____

_____

But the fruit of the Spirit is love, joy, peace, patience, kindness, goodness, faithfulness, gentleness and self-control,
–Galatians 5:22-23

Blessed are the poor in spirit, for theirs is the kingdom of heaven. Blessed are those who mourn, for they will be comforted. Blessed are the meek, for they will inherit the earth. Blessed are those who hunger and thirst for righteousness, for they will be filled. Blessed are the merciful, for they will be shown mercy. Blessed are the pure in heart, for they will see God. Blessed are the peacemakers, for they will be called sons of God. Blessed are those who are persecuted because of righteousness, for theirs is the kingdom of heaven.
–Matthew 5:3-10

Threatened Losses

Today's Objective:
You will learn how the fear of loss affects you and how to see your losses in the context of life experiences.

The most difficult losses of life often are the threatened losses. The possibility of their occurring is real, but you can do little about it. Your sense of control is destroyed.

For instance, let's say you have worked for 19 years at the same company. At 20 years, all benefits are secure. Then someone informs you that, due to a sluggish economy and lost contracts, the company will terminate 40 percent of its employees at the end of the month, and the length of employment is no criteria for being retained. Will you be one of the 40 percent?

Here are some of the other threatened losses in life:
- You wait for the outcome of a biopsy.
- Your spouse says, "I'm thinking of divorcing you."
- You make a business investment that may not come through.
- An angry employee or customer sues you.
- You are in a foreign country and the government threatens to retain everyone as hostages.
- A friend tells you he suspects your son has been using drugs for the past year.

✎ **Below name a threatened loss that you have experienced in your life.**

_____

_____

Did the loss occur? ❏ Yes ❏ No If so, how did you cope? If not, describe how you felt when the loss never materialized.

_____

_____

_____

Feeling helpless

We can do very little about potential losses, and we feel the loss before it occurs, even if it never actually materialized. Threatened losses make us feel helpless.

Even the delight of having a child brings accompanying losses. As one young mother put it: "I never realized all the adjustments having a baby would bring. My time is not my own, my energy is gone, my body is not my own, our intimacy and romance have been shelved, and I feel like a prisoner at home. I can't go out when I want to any more. I feel as if I've lost out on life!"

✎ **Have you experienced a loss that people usually would not categorize as a loss? If so describe this.**

_____

_____

These adjustments or losses are quite common. They can be anticipated and even planned for to ease their impact. But the majority of losses we experience are difficult to grieve, because we usually do not recognize them as losses.

Nina Hermann Donelly writes:

"The trouble with trying to mourn loss when death isn't involved is that there is no body, no funeral, and no public shoulder to cry on. There is no traditional, socially sanctioned outlet for mourning when the loss isn't death. Loss of function, relationship, or financial resources, for example, bring no printed obituary, no 'remains' laid to rest, no public gathering to cement the fact and focus love on the mourner. Trying to mourn loss when death is not involved is a lonely hell, with vague beginnings and endings defined more often by the intangible dimensions of lost and found hope than by the perimeters of the crisis itself."[2]

We all live with fear. Some of us live with more fear than others do. Every loss we experience from early infancy on becomes part of this pool of fear within us. We are afraid of misfortune, and we tend to avoid those who have experienced it for fear it might be contagious.

✎ **Have you ever avoided someone who experienced loss for fear that it might rub off on you? If so, describe this experience.**

_____

_____

One person wrote: "I avoided a friend who suffered a miscarriage for fear that the same thing would happen to me when we decided to have children. I now realize that I could have been a support for her and that my pulling away hurt her." Or, "I shunned a friend whose company laid him off because I was so insecure about my own work situation."

When we suffer loss, we tend to focus only on the present moment. We need to learn to view loss as a part of the bigger picture of our lives. Jesus sometimes experienced loss—right in the middle of a time of joy and purpose. At the marriage celebration in Cana, Jesus surely must have felt sadness at realizing that His family did not understand Him. This sadness came in the context of a joyous celebration and the joy of being about His Father's business as He turned the water into wine. He experienced the loss of Lazarus coupled with the joy of knowing that He would raise His friend from death and do the will of His Father. In the verses appearing in the margin read about these two incidents.

✎ **After reading the verses appearing in the margin about the two events described, answer this question: How do you think Jesus saw these losses in the context of His entire life?**

_____

_____

_____

On the third day a wedding took place at Cana in Galilee. Jesus' mother was there, and Jesus and his disciples had also been invited to the wedding. When the wine was gone, Jesus' mother said to him, "They have no more wine." "Why do you involve me?" Jesus replied, "My time has not yet come."... Nearby stood six stone water jars, the kind used by the Jews for ceremonial washing, each holding from twenty to thirty gallons. Jesus said to the servants, "Fill the jars with water"; so they filled them to the brim....The master of the banquet tasted the water that had been turned into wine.... This, the first of his miraculous signs, Jesus performed in Cana of Galilee. He thus revealed his glory, and his disciples put their faith in him.

–John 2:1-11

When Mary reached the place where Jesus was and saw him, she fell at his feet and said, "Lord, if you had been here, my brother would not have died." When Jesus saw her weeping, and the Jews who had come along with her also weeping, he was deeply moved in spirit and troubled. "Where have you laid him?" he asked. "Come and see, Lord," they replied. Jesus wept.... Jesus, once more deeply moved, came to the tomb. It was a cave with a stone laid across the entrance. "Take away the stone," he said.... So they took away the stone.... Jesus called in a loud voice, "Lazarus, come out!" The dead man came out.... Jesus said to them, "Take off the grave clothes and let him go."

–John 11:32-44

Jesus could withstand these losses because He knew what God had in store for Him. He knew that God was greater than the circumstances. We too can have that same assurance. We may not be able to see the path ahead clearly, and we may not fully understand life's twists and turns—some of them devastating—but we know that God wants good things for us, as our memory verse suggests. He can see our loss in context of a larger picture, and we can have faith that we too will understand that picture someday, even if we don't at the moment.

We know that God wants good things for us.

✎ **Say aloud your memory verse, Proverbs 3:5-6. How do you feel when you read the Bible promise that God will direct your paths and be in charge of your future?**

_____

_____

During the experience of loss, you may find you need to address hidden questions at some point. Some of these questions are:

- Will life go on for me despite this loss? Will I recover?
- Can I continue with my life without whatever or whomever has been lost to me? Should I feel guilty for doing so?
- Can I live a fulfilled life knowing that the person I've lost really is gone and that things will now be vastly different for me?

✎ **Can you think of some other hidden questions that you may need to address? Below list them.**

_____

_____

In succeeding chapters we will attempt to answer some of these questions.

Weekly Work

✎ **Review this week's lessons. Pray and ask God to help you identify one positive statement that had an impact on your understanding of your loss. Write that statement in your own words.**

_____

_____

Notes

[1]R. Scott Sullender, *Losses in Later Life* (New York: Paulist Press, 1989), 3, adapted.

[2]Nina Hermann Donelly, *I Never Know What to Say* (New York: Ballantine Books, 1987), 123.

Losses We Never Considered

SEPARATING THE LOSSES

Ken shared this testimony with his support group: "Just after our family made its last move, I was involved in a traffic accident while I attempted to find the post office in our new town. A car ran into me because I didn't realize that the street didn't have a turning lane like the streets in my previous town did. It made me realize that loss of familiar surroundings is a secondary loss that is a spin-off of my initial loss of location."

How will what Ken learned from this traffic accident help him move toward a more rapid recovery from the loss of his hometown? In this unit you will read more about this process.

Case in point

What you'll learn

This week you will

- identify secondary losses that result from your initial loss;
- describe ways the loss of identity connected to your loss compounds the struggle to recover;
- discover that who you are in Christ is far more important than is your identity based on a relationship to someone or something;
- learn the importance of resolving childhood losses so that you can cope with adult losses in a more emotionally healthy way;
- decide to put your trust in Jesus Christ rather than feeling that you must always be in control.

What you'll study

Secondary Losses	Loss of Identity	The Source of Our Identity	Childhood Losses	Who's In Control?
DAY 1	DAY 2	DAY 3	DAY 4	DAY 5

Memory verse

This week's verse of Scripture to memorize

If we confess our sins, he is faithful and just and will forgive us our sins and purify us from all unrighteousness.

—1 John 1:9

Today's Objective:
You will identify secondary losses that result from your initial loss.

Secondary Losses

We make further progress in recovering from our loss when we identify the "secondary losses" that result from the initial loss. These can be actual visible losses or can be subtle changes involving our relationships, status, environment, living style, hopes, dreams, wishes, and fantasies.

 In the following five paragraphs underline losses with which you can identify or which you have experienced.

One of my students lost his older brother in a traffic accident. This older brother had been responsible for caring for their elderly parents. But now this brother was gone, and this student felt that he should take over the care of his parents. This caused him to drop out of school, delay his education, change vocational direction, postpone additions to his own family, and limit his time with his wife, child, friends, and hobbies. Do you see all the secondary losses involved?

Entire groups can experience a loss. When a highly loved minister leaves his congregation after 15 years, the whole congregation experiences grief and all the accompanying stages.

A loss is associated with anticipating an achievement that never occurs. At the end of a major sports event, athletes on the losing team hang their heads in sorrow or weep silently. Politicians cry in front of cameras after defeat in an election. They not only lost the election, they lost pride, anticipated income, and self-worth. All these were losses of anticipated gains. The contenders never really had what they lost, but this doesn't make their grief any less real.

The loss of an ideal creates a powerful type of grief. On November 22, 1963, when news arrived that President Kennedy was shot and killed, the entire nation entered into a collective mourning process.

Loss of the familiar

How many times in your life have you changed residences? A move involves more than merely relocating. It includes the loss of all of our old niches—familiar routines, neighbors, hairdresser, shopping malls, auto mechanics, doctors. But we often don't recognize a move as being a major loss for us.

 Below write about how you have coped with one of the losses you underlined.

_____

_____

_____

Ken, who identified readily with the paragraph about moving, answered this way: "Just after our family made its last move, I was involved in a traffic accident while I attempted to find the post office in our new town. A car ran into me because I didn't realize the street didn't have a turning lane like the streets in my previous town did. It made me realize that loss of familiar surroundings is a secondary loss that is a spin-off of my initial loss of location."

Having a disease such as cancer is considered a major loss because of the health change. But have you considered all of the additional secondary losses? Some are physical and some symbolic. A person loses a familiar home environment because she must stay in a hospital room. A person loses independence because of the illness and because he must rely on others for care.

But these are not all of the losses involved. A disease such as cancer has a devastating and often numbing effect on its victims. A cancer patient may experience a loss of autonomy, bodily functions, body parts, predictability, pleasure, identity, intimacy, hope, job, enjoyable hobbies, social interaction or contacts, self-esteem, and possible loss of mobility.

Compounding the loss

Every lesser loss a person experiences compounds the overall feeling of loss. And each loss needs a grief reaction. We need to mourn each loss. The meaning and extent of loss varies for each person, depending on how much we had invested in the relationship; thus the grieving required varies. The loss of a body part will greatly impact a person with cancer who always has been concerned with physical appearance. The change in work and recreational involvements may affect another person most, whereas the limited social contacts might have the greatest impact on another person.

The grieving loved one can benefit by identifying the secondary losses.

The death of a significant person is a major loss, but the grieving loved one can benefit by identifying the secondary losses as well. Such losses include the loss of hopes, dreams, wishes, fantasies, feelings, expectations, and needs. You lose not only the present but the future as well. A widow realizes that she no longer will have a partner with whom to share retirement, church functions, couples' groups, a child's wedding, a grandchild's first birthday, and holidays.

Most people, however, don't identify their losses separately. They don't break them down and grieve for each one. Unfortunately, this makes the grief more intense, and this can delay the recovery process and new attachments.

✎ **As a step toward your recovery, begin the process of identifying your losses separately. Complete the following exercise. You may need additional paper as you begin to list your secondary losses.**

The loss I currently struggle with is _____.

What else did I lose as a result of this major loss?

1. _____

2. _____

3. _____

4. _____

5. _____

❦ **Stop and pray. The process of identifying additional losses that you have sustained can be painful but can bring growth. Ask God to give you the courage and insight to continue in this process of looking at losses.**

Loss of Identity

Today's Objective:
You will describe how the loss of identity connected to your loss compounds your struggle to recover.

Identifying some of the roles that the person who is lost to you played in your life may help you understand the direction your life now will take. Think of someone close you have lost—to death, to the breakup of a marriage, or even to a move or to the breakup of a friendship, and complete the exercise below.

 Circle any of the following terms that describe the relationship that the person has to you, and list additional roles we have not mentioned here.

friend	mechanic	daughter	prayer partner
handyperson	encourager	parent	source of
lover	business partner	brother	inspiration
gardener	bill payer	sister	or insight
companion	errand person	provider	teacher
sports partner	tax preparer	cook	counselor
checkbook	spouse	confidant(e)	protector
balancer	son	mentor	other _____

A personal loss

Seven months before I started writing this book, I experienced one of the major losses of my life. My son Matthew died. He was 22 years old and was profoundly mentally retarded. Throughout his life my wife and I experienced losses. The dreams and hopes I had for a son were lost. Even being able to hear him call me "Daddy" wasn't a reality, except for once or twice. The personal fulfillment of selecting a Christmas and birthday gift for him each year was lost, for he would respond to or use very little. We gradually got used to these losses and accepted them. But when Matthew died, an entirely new set of losses occurred in our lives. We no longer could look through the catalogs to select his special sleepwear; nor could we stop by Salem Christian Home (where he lived for his last 11 years) to take him out to lunch. We experienced the future loss of not having Matthew home on Thanksgiving or Christmas. And little additional unanticipated losses occur weekly. We don't call the home anymore to see how he's doing, a subject of conversation is gone. My wife and I must face and grieve over each loss in order to move on with our lives.

My wife and I must face and grieve over each loss in order to move on with our lives.

In *Treasures from the Dark,* pastor Ike Reighard wrote about the death of his wife, Cindy. Not only did Reighard identify Cindy as his best friend, he also called her a source of his spiritual strength. He wrote: "One night in the early weeks after Cindy died, I...sat at my desk trying to prepare a sermon for Sunday morning. After finally starting to concentrate on the message...I thought of a Scripture I wanted to use but couldn't remember the reference. Cindy always had a commanding knowledge of the Scripture; so out of habit, I spun around in my chair and called out, 'Cindy, where do you find—?' My voice suddenly halted as the brutal truth struck me once again. Cindy will not answer me. Not tonight, not ever again."[1]

Part of grieving each loss is developing an attitude of gratitude for the fact that you had a relationship with this person or thing in the first place. Stop and pray, thanking God that even in the midst of your sorrow you can acknowledge the good that came from these experiences.

Many of these losses that I mentioned above pertained to roles we had with Matthew, and now that part of our identity is lost. What identity losses have you sustained as a result of your loss? Too often we think that striving for identity is merely an adolescent search. But it isn't. Think about it for a minute. On what do you base your identity? Do you define yourself by your role or what you do? Do you build who you are upon your emotional attachments to other people, places, and things? People quite typically do this, and that would be fine if life were static, certain, predictable. But it isn't.

✎ **Take a moment and write your response to the question, "Who are you?"**

_____

_____

Defining myself

How much of that identity is related to the person or thing or situation you lost?

_____

As you answered the first question, did you discover yourself expressing certain roles in your life? I often hear expressions such as, "I am a man," "I am a father," "I am a social worker," "I am a minister," "I am a family person," "I am an athlete." But if you couldn't express who you are with these roles, what would you say?

At one of my seminars, I frustrate people because I ask them to introduce themselves to those around them and tell who they are, but they cannot mention what they do for a living. Just that simple instruction puts many of them into a state of conflict. If we do not have a broad basis for our identity, any kind of loss puts us into identity confusion. We have a mini identity crisis with each element that is taken away.

We have a mini identity crisis with each element that is taken away.

Think for a minute about these questions.
Who will I be when I no longer…
• am a father or mother?
• am a social worker (substitute your occupation)?
• have children living at home?
• am a family person?
• am an athlete?
• hold a particular office in an organization?

If we have no sense of who we are beyond our different roles in life, we have confined ourselves to a state of future identity confusion. However, we can avoid this loss.

✎ **Continue with this line of questioning to yourself. This time, write your own answers beside the questions.**

Isolating our losses

Who are the people to whom you are attached for your source of

identity? _____

_____

What are the things to which you are attached for your identity?

_____

_____

Does your identity fluctuate based on how well you believe you look?
❏ Yes ❏ No

Does how you feel about yourself fluctuate based on how well you believe you performed? ❏ Yes ❏ No

When we build our identity on anything that is potentially changeable, we set ourselves up not only to experience the losses themselves but the potential loss of our identity as well. Perhaps this startling fact will help you understand why the secondary losses often go well beyond the main loss you feel. We'll study more about this in day 3.

❧ Stop and pray. Ask God to strengthen you as you begin to recognize your secondary losses and how they contribute to the struggle you feel. Ask Him for the courage to grieve each of these losses one by one.

❧ Begin to memorize this week's memory verse. Say it aloud three times. Refer to page 21 if you need to refresh your memory.

DAY 3

Today's Objective:
You will discover that who you are in Christ is far more important than is your identity based on your relationships to someone or something.

The Source of Our Identity

Let's look at some other ways that our identity becomes involved in major losses in our lives.

The empty-nest stage of the family life cycle is a time when people feel losses keenly. The atmosphere of the home changes. Parents who are empty-nested have fewer choices to make and have less confusion and noise. Patterns of shopping, cooking, and scheduling will change. If a husband and wife relied on the children to hold their relationship together, the leaving of the last child creates an enormous loss within the marital relationship as well.

The mother who has relied on her role as the primary source of her self-identity may end up feeling abandoned, unloved, and depressed. If she gave up a career to have children, the loss of the last child can elicit resentment. It also can bring to light the fact that intimacy has been absent in the marriage; the camouflage no longer is there. The empty nest also affects fathers. A child who was mother's little girl at six may have become Dad's special pal. When she leaves, he could feel devastated. A child's leaving also points out to him that life could be passing him by too fast.

The person who for years has devoted his or her life to pursuing a dream through vocation finally hits a brick wall. Sometime in mid-life that person realizes that he or she never really will attain the goal and fulfill the dream. Or maybe this person arrives at the goal and says, "So what? Doesn't life have more meaning than this? Is this all?" A sense of loss and emptiness sets in.

Work and self-worth

Work often becomes the basis of our self-esteem or self-worth. Self-esteem increases when we feel good about what we accomplish on the job. Work may be more than a source of income. Work also is a source of social life, of status or prestige, or an opportunity to express yourself, to serve others, and to fill time. What happens when work is taken away? With a changing economy, foreign competition, and failing financial institutions, no profession or job is absolutely secure. A small recession occurs, and your company car is recalled, your office vanishes, your sales territory is re-shaped. Then how do you feel about yourself? These losses can be devastating.

Retirement can result in loss of self-esteem, social life, status or prestige, creativity of expression, opportunity to serve others, and time fulfillment. The meaning that you attach to work will determine how you respond to retirement. Some retirees I counsel are devastated and some aren't. It all goes back to the meaning they attached to their work.

Retirement is just one of the things that bring on an identity loss. A major identity loss facing many older people occurs when they sell a home that they have lived in for many years.

My mother moved to California in 1918 and built her first home in the hills above Hollywood. She subsequently built three other homes and lived there until 1978. But she still retained one of her houses—the one in which I grew up. Because she was one of the pioneers who settled in Laurel Canyon, and because she built two homes with her own hands and kept those homes in repair for almost 60 years, her identity was wrapped up in her property and homes. When she finally came to the time in her life to sell, it was the final step in an identity transition. She no longer was a resident or a home owner in Laurel Canyon. Her identity now is tied in to a retirement community.

When you live in a home for more than half a century, the move is much more than shifting from one house to another. You have lived out many roles there. You have experienced the major issues and changes of life there. Your history is tied into the home. Moving, voluntarily or otherwise, means being uprooted.

✎ **Go back to the paragraphs you just read about loss of identity. Underline losses with which you can identify or have experienced. Below write about how you have coped with one of these identity losses you underlined.**

_____

_____

_____

_____

One person wrote: "When my company laid me off, I thought I would lose my mind. For years I had been successful in my business and had climbed higher and higher in my profession. Without my name plate on my door, I felt stripped of everything. I felt I was nothing if I could not be the vice president. I coped very badly and in my devastation said some harmful things to my family."

Who are you, really?

But losing a loved one, a job, a role, or a dream does not have to cause us to lose our identity. We can cope better with our losses if we learn the true source of our identity. The question is not, "Who are you in light of your work, home, role as a parent, or relationship to someone you lost?" The issue is who you are spiritually. The question is, "Who are you, really?" And the answer you can build a life on is, "His!" You belong not to yourself. You belong to Him.

In *Search for Significance* LIFE® Support Group Series Edition, Robert S. McGee writes that our value does not depend on our ability to achieve or to perform. The true source of our identity is God's love and acceptance, which are unchanging. He created us. He alone knows how to fulfill all of our needs.

Money, fame, houses, success in a job, or our role as spouse, parent, or friend are only counterfeits of the true worth we have in Christ. Though these promise to meet our need for fulfillment, the things they provide are short-lived. God and His purposes alone can give us a profound, lasting, sense of significance.[2]

I have come that they may have life, and have it to the full.
–John 10:10

If we confess our sins, he is faithful and just and will forgive us our sins and purify us from all unrighteousness.
–1 John 1:9

✎ **Read the two verses appearing at left. What do these two verses tell you about how highly Christ regards you?**

_____

_____

John 10:10 reminds us of how much God treasures His creation. It reminds us that Christ came to earth so that people might experience life fully. Our memory verse for the week, 1 John 1:9, reminds us that Christ came to earth to save us and that He forgives us of our sins when we ask for forgiveness. How much more can we be treasured than that?

✎ **How do you feel when you realize that God regards you this highly?**

_____

_____

_____

_____

We will deal with our losses so much better when our identity is in Christ and we see ourselves from God's perspective—valued, loved, and sufficient because of Him.

Does this mean that you're not supposed to grieve for the person, object, or situation that you have lost? Certainly not! Your loss is profound; don't try to minimize it. But realizing that you are no less of a person without that object of your love or attachment will help give you the strength to recover.

🐣 **Stop and pray, thanking God for His immense love for you. Ask Him to help you depend on Him and not on other people or things as the source of your significance.**

DAY 4

Today's Objective:
You will learn the importance of resolving childhood losses so that you can cope with adult losses in a more emotionally healthy way.

Childhood Losses

As we mentioned briefly in unit 1, the unresolved losses of our childhood may compound the losses of our adult life. The losses vary in their complexity and their intensity. For example some children are never allowed to grieve over the death of a favorite pet. Adults tell them, "Don't cry. It's just a cat," or "We'll get you a new one tomorrow," or "Big boys (or girls) don't cry."

Sometimes parents withdraw their involvement from a child without explaining why. Both of John's parents supported him in all his soccer, softball, and school activities, but when he turned 11, they with no explanation stopped attending his activities. They didn't even ask him about them. He ached for some response on their part. This disappointment led him to fear that "everyone will end up doing this to me."

 What do you suspect might happen to John if he as an adult lost someone close to him through death , divorce, or other circumstances?

_____

_____

John might have difficulty grieving an adult loss because of pent-up anger and disappointment about this early loss in his life. Losing someone close to him might compound John's sense that "everyone leaves me eventually anyway." He may abandon others as a way to avoid being abandoned. Individuals like John need to grieve their early losses not only so they can deal with later losses but also so that their adult relationships can be more healthy.

Losses from divorce

More and more people enter adulthood with a sense of loss because they were children of divorce. In divorce, children can experience not only the disruption of the family but also the possible permanent loss of a home, neighborhood, school friends, standard of living, and family outings.

When a parent dies, a child experiences a sense of closure to the relationship and an opportunity to say a final good-bye. The child goes through a rather predictable period and sequence of mourning. But where is the mourning period after divorce? It is open-ended. It comes and goes, depending on the involvement of the noncustodial parent. If the parent does not stay involved, a child feels, *Is Mom (or Dad) ever coming back? If not, why not? What did I do wrong to cause this?* The occasional birthday card, the weekly phone call, and the all-too-infrequent visits and vacations keep the fantasy that the parent might return. (For additional information on this see my book, *Always Daddy's Girl*, and three books in the LIFE® Support Group Series: *A Time for Healing: Coming to Terms with Your Divorce*, for adults; *Healing the Wounds*, for teenagers, and *KidShare: What Do I Do Now?*, for children.

Physical and sexual abuse of children are damaging losses that contaminate adulthood. They destroy children's sense of innocence and security, and violate their perception of adults. Such children often learn to suffer silently. They have lost the love of a parent, their dreams, and their sense of innocence. They have lost out on their childhood!

Other children suffer damage—both physical and emotional—because of abandonment. Often children cannot understand why they feel so alone and abandoned. They know their parents meet their physical needs but neglect their emotional needs. Such children do not experience nurturing, hugging, or emotional intimacy. Soon they begin to wonder, *What is wrong with me?* They carry their perception with them throughout their adult lives.

Time alone will not heal those wounds because the memory has such a foothold.

When we identify and confront the losses of childhood, the process of letting them go is anything but passive. It is a very active endeavor. Time alone will not heal those wounds because the memory has such a foothold. It will take all the steps of grieving, letting go, and saying good-bye that the rest of this book mentions. You may need to participate later in a support group to concentrate on grieving those childhood losses. (See the Unit 6 segment, "Where Do I Go from Here?" for suggestions about some next steps you can take.)

✎ **What do you think might happen when an adult loses a parent who was abusive or neglectful? What will happen to that adult's grieving process?**

_____

_____

_____

Such a person may have unresolved anger toward the deceased parent or may feel numb, indifferent, or unable to feel the loss. The individual may even feel glad that the parent has died. This can set the individual up for guilt feelings that will cause regret later. Thus feelings of continual loss will set in.

Continual loss

I remember a day when the sadness of a continual loss hit me again. At the time, our retarded son was 17. A friend shared with me that he had taken his six-year-old son on an overnight camping trip. As the friend discussed his excitement and delight, part of me was happy with him, but another part was very uncomfortable. I even wished he would stop telling me about the trip.

I soon realized what was happening. I once again was feeling a sense of loss. I wished I had been able to experience those things with my son, but I never would. Matthew's limited capabilities would not allow this experience to be one he and I would share together. I felt the loss once more, and a sense of sadness was with me for the entire day. The sadness lifted the next day, and I had changed because of that brief experience. I could deal with the loss because I was an adult and understood the complexity of losses, grief, and God's compassion and comfort. Not so with children who experience loss repeatedly. Their abilities are limited, and they become very susceptible to recurring hurt, sadness, and depression.

Think about your life as a child. Have you identified the losses? Do they loom out of proportion to all of your experiences and affect the way you perceive all of your life?

Think about the losses you expect to experience within the next 5 to 10 years.

What about the losses you expect to experience in the next 5 to 10 years? You may know that within 5 to 10 years you likely will retire, change jobs, relocate, or have an empty nest at home. You may know that within that time frame you likely will lose a loved one. How you respond to losses today and tomorrow may result from how you respond to the early losses in your life.

✎ **Answer the following questions. You may need to use additional paper for your answers.**

Reflect on one of the earliest significant losses in your life. When did it occur? How old were you? Where was it? Who were the people involved? What actually happened?

_____

_____

How did you react to the loss?

_____

Did anyone suggest to you or advise you how to deal with the loss?

_____

What did you learn then that may be hindering the way you cope with loss today?

_____

What did you learn about loss at an early age that helps you today?

_____

_____

Based on what you learned from this lesson as well as from the previous loss, describe one thing you will do to respond in a more healthy way to the next loss you encounter.

_____

_____

Do not be afraid; you will not suffer shame. Do not fear disgrace; you will not be humiliated. You will forget the shame of your youth.

–Isaiah 54:4

✎ **Read the Scriptures appearing in the margin. How can the promises of these two verses help free you from the hold the past has on you—a hold that interferes with your coping?**

_____

_____

The Lord is the Spirit, and where the Spirit of the Lord is, there is freedom.

–2 Corinthians 3:17

With God's help, you can acknowledge and grieve the losses that you sustained in childhood. You can forget the shame. God does not promise that you will forget the incident or the pain, but He can free you from the chains of the past that bind you.

❦ **Stop and pray. Ask God to remove those chains that keep you from fully grieving your current loss. Ask Him to continue to give you courage to grieve your losses one at a time.**

Who's in Control?

Today's Objective:
You will decide to put your trust in Jesus Christ rather than feeling that you must always be in control.

Every loss is important. Loss is part of life, and we cannot avoid it. We grow by losing and then accepting the loss. Life takes on a deeper and richer meaning because of losses. The better we deal with them, the healthier we become and the more we grow. No one said that loss was fair, but it is a part of life.

Perhaps loss traumatizes us so much because it carries with it the message: "You really are not in charge of your life. You don't have much control over your destiny. You are at the mercy of whatever happens."

We all like to be in control of our lives—or at least we like to think we are. Loss of control is one of our most common fears. The things we value most are the very things we believe we must have control over: power, prestige, a person, a job, status, an object, a situation, and so on. You can take charge of some losses; you can create and orchestrate them. A woman who quits her job believes she retains some control over her career, even though the aspect of loss still is present. But if the company fires her, the loss is greater because she has lost control.

 Think of a time in your life when you experienced a loss of control such as an illness or job situation. Below describe the incident, and describe how you felt in that circumstance.

_____

_____

_____

We react with controlling behavior because we fear trusting others.

All of us have experienced instances in which we were not in control. Loss of control is painful for anyone, but some of us become particularly controlling because we fear the control, influence, or direction of others. We react with controlling behavior because we fear trusting others. We fear not being in charge of our own destiny or direction in life.

If we are people with rigid personalities, such as highly dominant, controlling people or perfectionists, we will have extra difficulty dealing with loss. Controlling people do not have much flexibility. Instead of being resilient, they are brittle. The more unexpected the loss, the more trouble they have. Setbacks cause them to make adjustments and changes. Besides their rigidity, they lack a wide range of coping skills, and this makes the problem worse.

 In the following three paragraphs underline words or phrases that you believe describe you and your need to control.

Dr. Lloyd John Ogilvie said about controlling people: "I wonder how controllers like these get along with God. I wonder how they learn to trust Jesus Christ as Savior. I wonder how they try to determine God's will for their lives (or maybe that question never enters their minds). I wonder how controllers handle the unexpected and uncontrollable losses of life and learn to view these upsets with a spiritual perspective. A controller cannot trust God because he fears the control of his life resting in anyone's hands but his own."

On the issue of control and fear as it relates to spiritual life, Ogilvie states: "Our need to be in charge of ourselves, others, and situations often makes our relationship with Christ life's biggest power struggle. We are reluctant to relinquish our control and allow Him to run our lives. We may believe in Him and be active in the church and Christian causes, but trusting Him as Lord of everything in life can be scary. Even though we pray about our challenges and problems, all too often what we really want is strength to accomplish what we've already decided is best for ourselves and others.

"Meanwhile, we press on with our own priorities and plans. We remain the scriptwriter, casting director, choreographer, and producer of the drama of our own lives, in which we are the star performer."[3]

You may have underlined such phrases as *reluctant to relinquish our control, trusting Him as Lord of everything in life can be scary,* or *press on with our own priorities and plans.* Trusting another person—even God—is risky. Living by faith may be a new experience for you. But living a life of faith in Jesus Christ is far less risky than living a life of faith in yourself. Trying to control your life imprisons you in the need to be in control. Trusting in His control leads to a life of freedom rather than a life of slavery.

Living a life of faith in Jesus Christ is far less risky than living a life of faith in yourself.

✎ **Check the answer below that best describes your response to the statement that, "You can live a life of faith in Jesus Christ that enables you to entrust all matters of your life to Him."**

❑ I believe, but I struggle to really trust Christ.
❑ I have always tried to control life myself.
❑ Yes, trusting Jesus really works and I am learning to surrender more of my life to Him.
❑ I do not understand what "faith in Christ" is all about.
❑ Other _____

Turning your life over to Jesus Christ may be a new concept for you. You can ask God to forgive you for the times you took your life into your own hands, the times that you hurt others (or yourself), and for other sins in your life. The message of Christ's death and resurrection is a message of hope, healing, and cleansing. It is a reassurance that we can turn from our harmful ways and that He is faithful and just to forgive us, as this week's memory verse says.

If we confess our sins, he is faithful and just and will forgive us our sins and purify us from all unrighteousness.
–1 John 1:9

In Acts 16:31, Luke wrote, "Believe in the Lord Jesus, and you shall be saved." If you have not done so already, you can receive Jesus Christ right now by invitation. If you want to trust Christ and accept His payment for your sins and turn your life and your trust over to Him, tell that to God in prayer right now. You may use the sample prayer below to express this commitment you've made.

Lord Jesus, I need You. I want You to be my Savior and my Lord. I accept Your death on the cross as payment for my sins, and I now entrust my life to Your care. Thank You for forgiving me and for giving me a new life. Please help me grow in my understanding of Your love and power so that my life will bring glory and honor to You. Amen

_____ (signature) _____ (date)

Trusting in Christ does not guarantee that your problems will instantly go away. It does not mean that you will immediately be free from the pain of your loss or that no more loss will occur in your life. It means that He forgives you, that you are starting a relationship with Him that lasts into eternity, and that He will grant you unconditional love and acceptance, as well as His strength, power, and wisdom, as you continue to grow in recovering from your loss.

A challenge to you

We need to remember this: we never were in total control! We are not in total control now! We never will be in total control! God is in control. Why stay enslaved to the myth that we must be in control? We have a better way to live. I wonder what would happen to us if we placed the control of our lives in Christ's hands for 30 days? It just might help us better deal with the losses of life.

✎ Can you commit to that kind of surrender? Would you be willing to turn the grief from your loss over to God for 30 days and see what wonders He can work in your life? If you would commit to do that, below write, "Dear God, I commit to turn my grief and despair over to you for 30 days. I will not suggest to you how you should fix things but will wait with eagerness to see what you will do in my life."

_____

_____

_____

✎ Check your memory work on this week's memory verse, 1 John 1:9. In the margin write it three times from memory.

❧ Stop and pray, asking God to give you the courage to surrender total control of your life to Him, even when your old patterns creep back in.

Weekly Work

✎ Review this week's lessons. Pray and ask God to help you identify one positive statement that had an impact on your understanding of your loss. Write that statement in your own words.

_____

_____

_____

Notes
[1]Dwight "Ike" Reighard, *Treasures from the Dark* (Nashville: Thomas Nelson, 1990), 152-153.
[2]Robert S. McGee, *Search for Significance* LIFE® Support Group Series Edition (Houston: Rapha Publishing, 1992), 19-20.
[3]Lloyd John Ogilvie, *Twelve Steps to Living Without Fear* (Dallas, Texas: Word Incorporated, 1987), 133.

The Meaning of Grief

Case in point

HOLDING BACK RECOVERY

On the surface, Greta seemed to cope well with her husband's death. She grieved openly about her loss and talked to friends about how much she hurt. But friends noticed that Greta took no steps to move on with her life. Even a year after his death, Greta had done little to assume financial responsibility for herself. She let bills pile up as if her husband would appear magically someday and begin balancing the checkbook and making financial plans for the family.

How will Greta's denial delay her recovery from the loss of her husband? In this unit you will read more about how denial can thwart the normal grieving process.

What you'll learn

This week you will
- discover why you need to enter into your grief fully in order to learn to live fully again;
- use a "programmed cry" to help you express your grief fully as a means of healing from your loss;
- learn about the feelings of depression, anxiety, hurt, and anger that loss generates and how to use these feelings effectively;
- describe defense tactics that people use to create a buffer against loss;
- begin to take charge of your grief by seeking the help of others and letting others know what they can do to help.

What you'll study

Replacing "Why?" with "How?"	The Role of Tears	Feelings that Loss Generates	Defense Tactics	Seeking Others' Help
DAY 1	DAY 2	DAY 3	DAY 4	DAY 5

Memory verse

This week's verse of Scripture to memorize
For as he thinks within himself, so he is.

—Proverbs 23:7, NASB

Replacing "Why?" with "How?"

Today's Objective:
You will enter into your grief fully in order to learn to live fully again.

A young wife shared how she felt when she found out that the baby she and her husband were planning to adopt would not be available to them because the birth mother had changed her mind. "I felt as though something had been ripped right out of me," she said. "It hurt so bad. I felt hollow inside."

A divorced father told me, "For the past 13 years, when my son has come to me for the weekend and I have to take him back to his mother, I grieve all over again. The pain comes back with all its intensity. It still cuts like a knife."

✎ **The two previous paragraphs contain descriptions of how grief affected these two persons. Below check any of the descriptions with which you can identity, or list any other descriptive statement that occurs to you.**

❑ "I felt as though something had been ripped right out of me."
❑ "I felt hollow inside."
❑ "The pain comes back with all its intensity."
❑ "It still cuts like a knife."
❑ _____

When you enter into grief, you enter into the valley of shadows. Grief is painful. It is work. It is a lingering process. But it is necessary for all kinds of loss. People have labeled it everything from intense mental anguish to acute sorrow to deep remorse.

A multitude of emotions involved in the grief process all seem out of control and often appear in conflict with one another. With each loss comes bitterness, emptiness, apathy, love, anger, guilt, sadness, fear, self-pity, and helplessness.

When grief is your companion, you experience it psychologically through your feelings, thoughts, and attitudes. It impacts you socially as you interact with others. You experience it physically as it affects your health and is expressed in bodily symptoms.

✎ **Has your grief impacted you socially or physically as the previous paragraph mentions? If so, describe below.**

_____

_____

One person responded: "I can be in the middle of a conversation with someone and suddenly my thoughts trail off to my loss. The person I'm talking to may think I'm ignoring her, but I mean no harm—my concentration simply hasn't returned yet. Or I can go to a party and try to have a good time, yet I feel sure that my grief is written all over my face."

Grief enters and exits your life without warning.

Grief enters and exits your life without warning. Grieving is not an abnormal response but is a normal, predictable, and expected reaction. In fact, not grieving is abnormal. Grief is your personal experience. Others do not have to agree with you that you've suffered a loss for you to experience grief.

Why grief?

Why grief? Why do have to go through this experience? What is the purpose? Through grief, you—
- express your feeling about your loss,
- express your protest at the loss as well as your desire to change what happened and have it not be true,
- express the effects you have experienced from the devastating impact of the loss.[1]

The purpose of grieving your loss is to get beyond these reactions to deal with your loss and work to adapt to it. The overall purpose of grief is to enable you to make the necessary changes so you can live with the loss in a healthy way.

When we experience loss, automatically we begin to ask the "Why?" question—"Why did this happen to me?" Asking "Why?" is a normal part of the grief process.

Pastor Ike Reighard, whose wife died during childbirth, wrote this about his questioning: "I hotly debated all of the whys of life and death in a way I'd never done before. I don't believe for a moment that it is unspiritual for a Christian to ask 'Why?' in experiences of heartbreak. I believe it is natural and honest … Although I have seen positive things come out of the death of Cindy and the baby, I've never really settled in my mind and heart why they died. Cindy loved and trusted God. The why questions that bombarded me at the time of Cindy's funeral persisted as I went about the business of trying to live without her. Why would He cut her life short? Why would He give us the baby and then take them both? It seemed downright stupid."[2]

We recover when we eventually can move from asking the Why? questions to asking, "How can I learn through this experience? How can I now go on with my life?"—a situation that Reighard says he ultimately progressed to. When the "How?" question replaces the "Why?" question, you start to live with the reality of the loss. "Why?" questions reflect a search for purpose in loss. "How?" questions reflect your searching for ways to adjust to the loss.

 Before you read any further about this process, score yourself on the scale below. Where do you think you are in your process of replacing the "Why?" questions with the "How?" questions? On the line make a vertical mark representing where you are in the process.

Where do you stand?

0	5	10
Still asking "Why?"	*Striving to adjust*	*More "How?"s than "Why?"s*

You may still be striving, but your eventual goal is to be able to say, as this writer did:

> This loss I've experienced is a crucial upset in my life. In fact, it is the worst thing that will ever happen to me. But is it the end of my life? No. I can still have a rich and fulfilling life. Grief has been my companion and has taught me much. I can use it to grow into a stronger person than I was before my loss.[3]

What do you have to do to get to this point? Can you take definite steps so you don't have to guess at the process? Follow these four steps.

1. Change your relationship with whatever you lost. For example, if you lost a spouse through death, you eventually can realize that the person is dead and you no longer are married to him or her. You recognize the change and develop new ways of relating to the deceased person. You learn to exist without the person the way you once learned to exist with the person. Memories, both positive and negative, will remain with you.
2. Develop your own identity and your life to reflect the changes that occurred because of your loss. This will vary, depending on whether the loss involved a job, an opportunity, a relationship, or a death.
3. Discover and take on new ways of functioning without what you lost. This involves a new identity without totally forgetting.
4. Discover new directions for the emotional investments you once had in the lost object, situation, or person.[4]

These steps may sound simple, but they are not, since all of grief involves work, effort, and pain. Let's consider how these steps can be accomplished.

Acknowledge and understand the loss. Depending upon the severity, some losses soon will be a faint memory while others, such as the death of a child or spouse, never may be completely settled. But this step does mean integrating the loss into your life. It means saying, "Yes, unfortunately this did happen." Facing your loss means you don't attempt to postpone the pain, you don't deny that it actually happened, and you don't minimize your loss. If you deny or minimize, you intensify your pain and drag it out. A common myth about grieving is that we should bury our feelings. Statements such as, "Don't cry," or "Don't feel bad" are damaging rules based on false ideas about grief. Often people make such unsupportive statements because they feel anxious about not knowing what to say. Making a list of all of the effects of your loss may help you face your pain. Feel and deal with all of your emotions.

A personal loss

✎ **Make a list of the effects of your loss. I have provided an example for you. You will need to use an extra sheet of paper for your list.**

All my children's baby pictures burned in the fire. I feel devastated.

_____

Tell others about your loss as soon as possible. Call it by its name: "It was a loss, and I am grieving." You may keep track of who you told, the date, and the person's response. Telling others means making the conscious decision that "I am going to face and feel the pain."

✎ **Below make a list of those you have told or need to tell about your loss. You will need extra paper to complete your list. I have provided an example for you.**

Who I Told	When	Response
1. my counselor	1. a week after I broke up with my fiance	1. encouraged me to cry; listened
2.	2.	2.
3.	3.	3.
4.	4.	4.

Surges of emotion

Sometimes people say they wish they could return to the initial stage of shock or numbness. At least at that point, the pain wasn't so intense. The numbness served as novocaine. Depending on the severity of your loss, your reaction can be a slight down feeling or an incapacitating numbness. Then in 24 to 36 hours it lifts, you face the pain, and the feelings surge. You will experience seasons of depression, anger, calm, fear, and eventually hope, but they don't follow each other progressively. They overlap and often are jumbled together. Just when you think you are over one, it bursts through your door again. You finally smile, but then the tears return. You laugh, but the cloud of depression drifts in once again. This is normal. This is necessary. This is healing.

Robert Veninga says: "There is one marvelously redeeming motive for entering fully into one's sorrow. Once you have experienced the seriousness of your loss, you will be able to experience the wonder of being alive."[5]

❧ **Stop and pray. Thank God for the people who helped and supported you after your loss. Ask God for the courage to help you enter fully into your sorrow so you truly can experience the wonder of life.**

Today's Objective:
You will learn how to use a "programmed cry" to help you express your grief fully as a means of healing from your loss.

He turned away from them and began to weep.

–Genesis 42:24

Deeply moved at the sight of his brother, Joseph hurried out and looked for a place to weep. He went into his private room and wept there.

–Genesis 43:30

The Role of Tears

Tears are the vehicle with which God has equipped us to express the deepest feelings words cannot express. We summon tears when in our weakness we cannot find words to express the deep emotions that we feel. Tears can express everything from jubilation to devastation. When words fail us, tears step in to help.

✎ **Can you identify with any of the words or phrases that the previous paragraph used to describe tears? In the previous paragraph circle anything that describes how you feel about the role of tears in your life.**

Many people identify with the phrases, "when words fail us, tears step in to help" or "in our weakness we cannot find words to express the deep emotions that we feel."

Genesis 42–50 is the account of Joseph's reunion with his brothers and his father after his brothers sold him into slavery. In his first encounter with his brothers, he told them one of them would have to stay in Egypt. As Joseph listened to them talking among themselves in his native language, his emotions surged to the surface. Read Genesis 42:24 in the margin about what Joseph did. Then when his brothers returned to Egypt with their youngest brother, the Bible tells about a second instance when Joseph wept. (See the second verse at left.) He wept uncontrollably again when his brother Judah made an offer to spare his father any more pain (Genesis 45:2).

The fourth occasion of Joseph's tears was after Joseph revealed his identity to his father and brothers. He also revealed his plan to bring them all to Egypt to live with him. At that point, Scripture says, "He threw his arms around his brother Benjamin and wept, and Benjamin embraced him, weeping." And then, "He kissed all of his brothers and wept over them" (Genesis 45:14,15). Three more times we have record of Joseph weeping: when his father arrived

When their message came to him, Joseph wept.

–Genesis 50:17

When Jesus saw her weeping, and the Jews who had come along with her also weeping, he was deeply moved in spirit and troubled. "Where have you laid him?" he asked. "Come and see, Lord," they replied. Jesus wept.

–John 11:33-35

in Egypt, when his father died 17 years later, and finally, when his brothers asked him to forgive them. Read the verse at left.

When words fail, tears are the messengers. Tears are God's gift to all of us to release our feelings. When Jesus arrived in Bethany after the death of Lazarus, He wept. See the second verse appearing in the margin.

✎ **Many people fear they will seem weak if they cry. As you read these verses about the tears of Joseph and Jesus, did you think Joseph and Jesus were weak?** ❑ **Yes** ❑ **No Why or why not?**

_____

_____

_____

Although some people may view tears as a sign of weakness, many people see the tears of Joseph and Jesus as showing their strength of character because they were not ashamed to show they cared for loved ones.

Ambushed by grief

The problem with tears is that you never know when they will emerge when you are grieving. When you experience a major loss in your life, you end up being ambushed by grief. I understand this statement far better now than I did when Matthew was alive. One morning it happened in our worship service. The service focused on Pentecost. As the organ played, suddenly the sound of a brass quartet filled the air. When Matthew was alive, he responded to the sound of trumpets. He would look up and reflect an alertness or wonderment in his expression, as if to say, "Oh, that's something new."

The sound of the brass in the service brought back another memory: Matthew's joyful laughter. Several years ago, I learned to play the trumpet. During one of Matthew's visits home, I took out the trumpet and began to practice. He looked at me with an expression that said, "I don't believe what I'm hearing!" He listened to another squawk, threw back his head, and laughed harder than we had ever heard him laugh. My novice attempts to play at least had pleased Matthew. Needless to say, these memories brought the tears once again.

Another time I was ambushed by grief when I was driving home and listening to Dr. Chuck Swindoll's radio program. During the message, he began to list the names of the disciples. When he said the name Matthew, it brought my sense of loss and sadness to the surface, where it stayed for several days. Who would have thought that would have happened!

✎ **As you've read these paragraphs, have you thought about a time you were ambushed by grief—when a sound or a sentence triggered grief when you least expected it? If so, below describe the situation.**

_____

_____

Sometimes the words of a familiar hymn bring on a flood of tears. Hymns that you may have sung hundreds of times and that contain words about the

"Dry" times in grief

We can overcome out dry times in grief by developing a "programmed cry."

Talk to God out loud

beauty and blessings of heaven suddenly can prompt tears because they may remind you that a loved one now is spending his or her eternity with God.

✎ **Has a familiar hymn ever caused you to weep? ❏ Yes ❏ No If so, in the margin box list hymns that have caused you to weep unexpectedly.**

Then I have times when my feelings are just flat. I feel a low-grade numbness, and I wonder when the pain will hit. Just three months after Matthew died, I had been very busy with projects. For several days, I had felt very little and had not cried. Then as I shared with a client what had happened, tears came to my eyes. On another occasion, as I sat with the parents of a profoundly disabled child and attempted to help them, my own tears rose to the surface.

During this "dry time" as I refer to it, grief hit hard again. I was riding my exercycle and listening to a worship tape by Terry Clark. One of the songs was "I Remember." As I rode, I was working on our new catalog to be sent out to people who had attended our seminars over the years. I was wondering whether or not to mention in this publication anything about Matthew, since most of the people had heard our story about him. I had thought of saying, "For years we had prayed for Matthew to be whole. On March 15, God saw fit to make him whole." As I thought about this—and perhaps because of the music and the fact that I was planning to visit his grave for the first time—the flood began. The sense of loss was overwhelming, and I wept deeply.

✎ **Have you ever experienced a "dry time" in your own grief? Have you ever had a time of flat feelings that later was broken by a flood of tears? ❏ Yes ❏ No If so describe below.**

_____

_____

Some of us may have these dry times because we never have learned to cry. We live with fears and reservations about crying. We cry on the inside but never on the outside. One way to overcome this is through a "programmed cry." A programmed cry is not a one-time activity but something a person might use on a number of occasions, especially during the first few months after a major loss. Some people will find a programmed cry especially useful on an anniversary date of a loss. Here are some how to's:

1. Select a room in your house that has some sentimental value for you. You will need tissues, a stereo, and photographs of the person or object you lost, whether your loss was through a dating breakup, divorce, death, job loss, or life change.
2. Turn the lights down low and take the phone off the hook so you have no interruptions. Turn on the stereo either to tapes or to a radio station that plays mellow music. As you begin to feel sad, continue to think about your loss. Look at any photographs that help you remember what you once had or would have had. Recall the positive and intimate times. Express out loud what you are feeling, and don't put a restraint on your tears.
3. Put an empty chair in front of you and talk to the chair as if the person were there. Sometimes visiting the grave of someone you've lost through death can help you have a programmed cry as you talk to the person. Talk to God out loud about the loss. Tears and words can express feelings of sadness, depression, longing, anger, hurt, fear, and frustration. Some people find

that writing a letter to the person or to God can be an effective way to access buried emotions.

✎ **Below describe your plans for your programmed cry. Where will you be? What items will you have with you? When will you do this?**

_____

_____

Remember that in the midst of these feelings and their expression, healing and recovery are taking place. Focus on the positive feelings and thoughts that emerge, and say the thoughts aloud. Then put away all the reminders and symbols of your weeping. Share your experience with a friend, counselor, or support group, or write it in a diary. You probably will discover that your fear or resistance to crying has diminished. It will be easier the next time.

🐦 **Begin to memorize this week's memory verse. To refresh your memory, refer to page 35.**

🐦 **Stop and pray, asking God to give you courage to cry and express your grief fully as you realize that it is a major step toward your healing.**

DAY 3

Today's Objective:
You will learn about the feelings of depression, anxiety, hurt, and anger that loss generates and how to use these feelings effectively.

Feelings that Loss Generates

Feelings of depression are normal and healthy after the initial shock wears off. The brain responds both consciously and unconsciously to the loss; previous experiences of loss also influence our thought processes. Depression begins to develop, and the depth of it depends on the intensity of attachment we had to what we lost. Eventually the depression levels out, and we begin to recover.

The person who has had excessive losses in his or her life and has not learned to grieve may develop negative patterns of thinking. This may cause the person to hold on to the loss or to re-create it continually. Some people have been taught, "Don't hope, and you won't be disappointed" or "Expect the worst, and protect yourself." This can create the "runaway-train" syndrome of depression. Leaving a train parked on a downgrade without the brakes properly set leads to predictable consequences. As the train moves down the tracks, it picks up momentum and soon is out of control.

The power of negative thinking

✎ **As you have coped with your loss, has negative thinking been like a runaway train? Below describe how pessimism has affected you.**

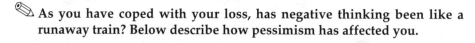

_____

One person wrote: "When my husband died, I believed that my life had ended as well. I expected bad things to happen to me, and they did. I stayed in and refused to go out with friends. Soon people stopped inviting me. I contributed to a self-fulfilling prophecy because of my pessimism. Much that had been enjoyable in my life was ending because of my negative thinking."

Sometimes depression gathers momentum because of:
- guilt
- self-blame
- negative self-talk
- distortions of reality
- misperceptions
- imagining additional losses.

The depression becomes self-perpetuating because we give it fuel. A college student who fails a major exam thinks, *I'll never pass this course, I don't have any ability, I didn't study the right way, I won't graduate, I won't get the job I want, My parents will think I'm a failure,* and so on. In time, this line of thinking would create depression in any of us. The depression becomes disproportionate to the loss.

For as he thinks within himself, so he is.
–Proverbs 23:7, NASB

✎ **This week's memory verse appears in the margin. How does this verse apply to you when you think about the ways you react to loss?**

_____

_____

If we become consumed with negative self-talk, then we become those things that we say to ourselves and say about ourselves. If we think, *I'm no good,* enough, our actions eventually bear out those thoughts.

Besides being tied to our positive or negative thoughts, recovery from loss is tied to our feelings. When we do not admit, face, and express our emotions, they become concealed. Withheld feelings lead to brittleness, vulnerability, and distorted perceptions.

Numerous studies show that a person's health risk is higher after a loss. You are more susceptible to heart attacks and cancer after the death of a loved one. A long-term study indicates that the death rate of widows and widowers is from two to seventeen times higher during the first year after the death of a spouse.[6] One reason for the higher death rate is because of a decrease in the body's immune system after a loss. But if a person does the work of grieving and doesn't postpone or avoid it, this immune system deficiency is avoidable.

The pain from a loss generates numerous feelings. One of these is anxiety. Anxiety is pain from an anticipated loss. It includes a wide variety of fears and worries. Some people who haven't yet experienced their loss in reality experience it in their thoughts, and the dread that comes on them is often as strong as if what they fear had occurred. Anxiety can be beneficial if you ask yourself what you are afraid of and why this is so important to you. Then you can prevent or minimize the loss.

What do I fear?

✎ **Complete the following exercise to get in touch with your anxiety.**

The fear I have related to my loss is _____

_____

Why am I so afraid of this happening? _____

_____

_____

What can I do to minimize my fear? _____

_____

One woman wrote: "The thing I fear most about having lost my job is that I'll look bad in the eyes of my parents. I fear this because my parents have always thought I could do no wrong, and the fact that I lost my job will embarrass them. I can minimize this fear by explaining the situation to my parents, believing in my own mind that I've done my best, and working diligently to make plans for my future."

Hurt is a core feeling of loss. It is pain in the present. What does it feel like? Sometimes it is sadness, sometimes disappointment, and sometimes depression. It feels as if you have been depleted. You are drained. You need to cope with hurt by expressing it.

✎ **In the margin box, begin to express your hurt. Complete the sentence, "I feel hurt because …"**

Someone completed the sentence this way: "I feel hurt because we had planned for two years to be married. All my hopes and dreams for our future are now in shambles because of my broken engagement."

Anger is a response to pain. The pain can be in the past, present, or future. When it is in the past, it is resentment. When direct expression is blocked, it leaks out and reveals itself elsewhere. If we direct our anger toward ourselves, it can become depression.

✎ **Have you directed your anger about your loss against someone else, or against yourself? Explain.**

_____

_____

You can start now to direct that anger properly. Complete the following:

What I'm really angry about concerning my loss is _____

_____

_____

You might have answered something like this: "I've taken my anger about the loss of my baby out against my boss. I've sulked on the job and been angry about work I had to do. All that does is endanger my job and put me at risk for an additional loss. What I'm really angry about is that we planned for this baby for five years and now we have to wait even longer to be parents."

❦ **Stop and pray the following prayer.**

Lord, I've been afraid to feel my emotions, or I have felt them improperly. I'm not afraid to admit that I do sometimes feel depressed, anxious, hurt, and angry about my loss. Help me to realize that I need to work through these stages before I can feel whole again. Amen.

I feel hurt because—

_____

_____

_____

_____

_____

_____

Defense Tactics

Today's Objective:
You will describe the five
defense tactics that can delay
your recovery.

We block healthy recovery in another way. We try to postpone the pain by creating a buffer against the feelings of sadness. Often we use some sort of defense tactic to gain time to adjust to the loss.

Some of us become experts with mental gymnastics—games that we use to deny, avoid, or defer an experience of loss. We are like ancient warriors who used shields to deflect enemy attacks. In this case, our enemy is the feeling of loss. We attempt to shield ourselves from the pain, but we simply prolong the accompanying pain. We may employ the following five methods in our attempt to negate the pain of loss. Though these methods are sometimes called stages of grief, we may experience them in any combination or order. They do not occur in any standard sequence.

1. Denial—When we experience rejection, abandonment, the loss of love, or even a death, denial is our first line of defense. Often we actually say, "No! That's not true. It can't be true!"

Denial is a common companion to loss. In fact, some people choose to live in a world of denial most of their lives. Those who were reared in emotionally dishonest families are gifted at this. They use denial to avoid emotionally recognizing that a loss has occurred or that it will occur. They compound the loss by not only denying the reality of what has occurred but also denying the results of the loss. I have seen denial in cases of loss of jobs, pets, persons, and even opportunities to go on to graduate school.

Denial occurs in many shapes and forms. People say to me, "Norm, I know in my head that this happened, but I feel as if it hasn't happened." They found the switch to turn off their emotions. In time, though, their emotions will catch up with their thoughts.

Many people live their lives as if a loss did not occur.

Another variation of denial is admitting the loss and feeling it but behaving as if it never occurred. Some have called this "third-degree denial." Many people live their lives as if a loss did not occur. If you ask them about it, they can talk about it and even shed tears over what happened, but their behavior contradicts their words.

On the surface, Greta seemed to cope well with her husband's death. She grieved openly about her loss and talked to friends about how much she hurt. But friends noticed that Greta took no steps to move on with her life. Even a year after his death, Greta had done little to assume financial responsibility for herself. She let bills pile up as if her husband would magically appear someday and begin balancing the checkbook.

✎ **How will Greta's denial delay her healthy recovery from her loss?**

_____

Can you think of ways you have used denial as a defense tactic in your recovery? ❏ **Yes** ❏ **No If so, describe.**

_____

The energy that we must expend to keep denial operating drains us.

Grieving involves moving through several levels of denial. Each stage brings home the reality of the loss a bit deeper and more painfully. We accept reality first in our heads, then in our feelings, and finally we adjust life's pattern to reflect the reality of what has occurred. We pay a price for prolonged denial. The energy that we must expend to keep denial operating drains us, and in time we can be damaged emotionally and delay our recovery.

2. In **rationalization**, someone might say, "It really didn't hurt that bad. I can find a better man out there. After all, I only went with him for two years." Or, "That job wasn't the best." Or, "Our neighborhood was changing anyway." Or, "Her death was for the best. She doesn't have to suffer any longer." Each of these statements has one basic purpose: to lessen the impact of the loss. But if a person lives with rationalization too long, he or she begins to believe it. It becomes a castle of protection to avoid the healing process. For example, while the person who has lost a loved one through death may be relieved that the loved one's suffering is over, the bereaved person will delay healing if he or she doesn't honestly grieve the loved one's loss as well and acknowledge its devastating impact.

✎ **Underline any of the statements in the above paragraph you may have used to rationalize your loss, or if none apply, write in the margin other rationalization statements you have used.**

3. **Idealization** distorts reality by overly glorifying what we lost. We overlook any negative characteristic or aspect, whether we are dealing with the loss of a job, death of a family member, or the move to a new city. A man made this comment about his alcoholic, physically abusive father, who recently died: "Dad was really a good provider for all of us, and in his own way, he really loved us." He refused to admit that his father had caused pain in his life.

In the healthy process of grief, this idealization soon recedes, and an accurate picture of the loss can occur. In an unhealthy situation, idealization often is so extreme that the grieving person will not allow anyone else to say anything bad or even realistic about the situation.

✎ **In the margin practice your objectivity by listing some positive and negative traits about the person or situation you lost. For example, you could describe how you loved the city from which you moved but also could acknowledge the problems you experienced there.**

4. A fourth defense is **reaction formation.** When a loss occurs, the person tends to run from the pain by overemphasizing the opposite of the present or impending pain. Have you ever faced an impending loss and tried to keep it from occurring by overreacting? A student who faces some failing grades may buckle down and study to change the impending loss—that is positive. But locking himself in his room, studying 12 hours a day, and missing meals and sleep is an overreaction. Fearing the loss of a relationship, one might become an overcompliant, submissive victim in a desperate attempt to hold on.

5. **Regression** is a way of avoiding pain by retreating to a younger way of behaving or even thinking. For example, a person whose husband leaves her regresses by entering a second adolescence. She might revert to a teen-age way of dressing and behaving in order to attract men because she thinks this will help her cope with her loss.

Some good aspects—

_____

_____

_____

Some aspects that were not so positive—

_____

_____

_____

✎ **Have reaction formation or regression become a part of your defense system for coping with loss?** ❏ Yes ❏ No **If so, describe below.**

_____

_____

If regression or any of these defense mechanisms become permanent fixtures in our lives, we do not eliminate the pain but simply lock it in as a barrier to growth and recovery. We can only experience recovery when we acknowledge the loss and grieve.

❦ **Stop and pray. Ask God to reveal to you any unhealthy barriers you may be constructing to coping with your loss.**

DAY 5

Today's Objective:
You will learn how to take charge of your grief by seeking the help of others and letting others know what they can do to help.

Friends I know I can count on—

_____

_____

_____

_____

Seeking Others' Help

You desperately need the support, help, and comfort of other people during your loss. You may think this is necessary only in the major losses of life, but, you need support in the smaller losses as well: a broken relationship, a child not being accepted into your alma mater, a lost pet, your inability to obtain a loan, or losing in a competition.

Isolation during a loss can be deadly. A friend can help you walk through the valley, take away your fear of abandonment, and help you to lift the depression. Other people can help you see that you can continue to function. They seem to loan their hope and faith when yours has vanished.

You may know intellectually that being with people is the best thing for you, but emotionally you may not feel like being with others. It may help to talk about your feelings with a nonjudgmental, caring, listening friend.

✎ **In the margin box write the initials of friends that you have identified with whom you can share your feelings.**

It may help to write down everything you are feeling and then express it. This is not a one-time experience. You will need to do it again and again. You have many forms of expression open to you.

✎ **Below circle the means of expression that you find most useful, or name other ways of expressing yourself that this list may not include.**

Running	Drawing
Walking	Sculpting
Aerobic exercise	Writing
Screaming	Other _____
Pounding on a bed	_____

Sometimes others, instead of merely listening to us, want to make things right. Instead of letting us pour out our souls as we cry, they immediately start suggesting things for us to do or places for us to go. Their acts, although well-meaning, don't always help. Sometimes we may need to say to friends: "During my recovery (or during this holiday, or this next few weeks) I may cry because I miss my wife (substitute your loss). When I do, don't become alarmed. Nothing is wrong with me. I don't need you to try to fix me. I just need you to listen and to be there for me."

As my wife and I grieved over the death of our son, people asked us how we were doing. We answered, "We're doing fine. We're grieving, crying, and feeling the loss." We said the additional words to let them know just what "doing fine" actually meant, since they might otherwise assume the tears had gone.

You may be uncomfortable with your grief. So might others around you. They want you "normal" as soon as possible, or they want you to act as if you are. But if you are not ready for it, others should not be the ones to determine when you are ready. This is your loss, not theirs. No one should rob you of your grief. Some may attempt to do that just because they are uncomfortable.

Life is a mixture of pain and joy. This is the time of pain. Most of us don't realize the pattern of peaks and valleys of grief. As part of her grief process, Sue drew a chart depicting the intensity of her feelings of grief. Her chart appears in the margin. Notice the jagged peaks. Typically, the pain and grief actually intensify at three months and then gradually subside but not in a steady fashion. They go up and down.

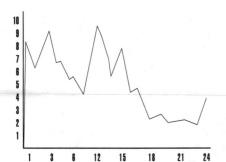

Below draw your own intensity-of-feelings timeline for the first two years of your grief or for the length of time since your loss.

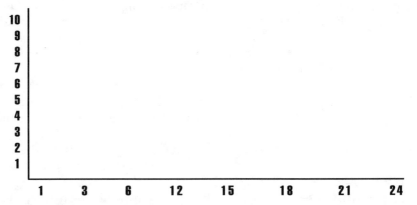

Most people don't need a reminder of the first-year anniversary of a devastating loss. The intensity of grief rushes in with pain that rivals the initial feelings of loss. If anyone attempts to tell you that you should be "over it by now" or "feeling better" at any of these times, you may become quite upset with them. That is understandable. It also is understandable that people lack an understanding of the process of grief unless they have been through it themselves. Share this chart with them and let them know how you are feeling and how normal feeling this way is.

You can take charge and let others know what you need and don't need at this time of your life. That doesn't always mean that others will comply, but they can try. Unfortunately you may have to educate them about grief. You have to go after what you need to resolve your loss. Let others know that they don't have to avoid bringing up your loss. Let them know you want them to call, to ask you how you are doing, and not to be put off by your tears or anger.

Perhaps you can help yourself and others by preparing a set of instructions to ease their anxiety and to assist you by responding in the most helpful fashion. Your group facilitator will give you a suggested letter that you can give to your family, pastor, friends, or co-workers. You can alter this letter to fit your loss situation. Copy the letter as many times as necessary.

Take charge of your grief. Face it. Experience it, and you will recover.

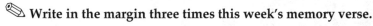 **Write in the margin three times this week's memory verse.**

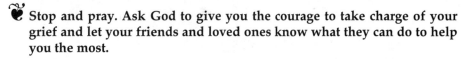 **Stop and pray. Ask God to give you the courage to take charge of your grief and let your friends and loved ones know what they can do to help you the most.**

Weekly Work

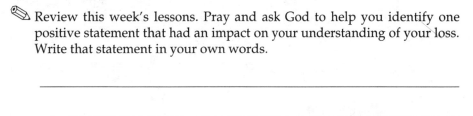 Review this week's lessons. Pray and ask God to help you identify one positive statement that had an impact on your understanding of your loss. Write that statement in your own words.

_____

_____

Notes

[1]Therese A. Rando, *Grieving: How to Go on Living When Someone You Love Dies* (Lexington, Mass.: Lexington Books, 1988), 11, 12, adapted.

[2]Dwight "Ike" Reighard, *Treasures from the Dark* (Nashville: Thomas Nelson Publishers, 1990), 67-68.

[3]Bob Deits, *Life After Loss* (Tucson: Fisher Books 1988), 27, adapted.

[4]Rando, 19, adapted.

[5]Robert Veninga, *A Gift of Hope* (Boston: Little, Brown and Company, 1985), 71.

[6]Deits, 103, , adapted.

Obstacles to Recovery

Case in point

What you'll learn

This week you will
- identify five types of unresolved grief that can disturb normal recovery from a loss;
- describe four more types of unresolved grief and how to spot them in your life;
- discover eight reasons that unresolved grief occurs;
- identify four more reasons for unresolved grief;
- learn 11 steps to take when you're stuck in your grief.

What you'll study

Types of Unresolved Grief	Unresolved Grief, Part 2	Reasons for Unresolved Grief	More Reasons	Help for People Who Are Stuck
DAY 1	DAY 2	DAY 3	DAY 4	DAY 5

Memory verse

This week's verse of Scripture to memorize
The Spirit helps us in our weakness. We do not know what we ought to pray for, but the Spirit himself intercedes for us with groans that words cannot express.

—Romans 8:26

DAY 1

Today's Objective:
You will identify five types of unresolved grief that can disturb normal recovery from a loss.

Types of Unresolved Grief

Several factors can disturb our recovery from a loss. We call the result "unresolved grief." The factors that lead to unresolved grief include grief that is: absent, inhibited, delayed, conflicted, or displaced.

In **absent grief** people do not exhibit feelings of grief and mourning over loss. They act as though the loss never occurred. They deny reality. Sometimes they minimize—they recognize the feelings of grief but minimize those feelings. They dilute the feelings through a variety of rationalizations. They attempt to prove that the loss does not really impact them. Minimizers may talk about how they already are back to their normal routines. "It doesn't hurt that much," they say.

This person often believes grief is something to think through quickly but not to feel. Words may become a substitute for expressing true feelings. Any feelings of grief threaten the minimizer, who seeks to avoid pain at all costs. However, the repressed feelings of grief continue to build internally. With no outlet, emotional strain and tension result.

Inhibited grief

Inhibited grief involves repressing of some of the normal grief responses. Other symptoms may take their place. Stomach aches, loss of energy, or headaches are some of the more common results. The grieving person may be able to grieve only about certain aspects of what he or she lost.

For almost a year after her mother died, Nancy shrugged off her loss but was constantly ill. For one whole week stomach cramps kept her from work; for many weeks she was unable to teach her Sunday School class because she had repeated headaches and colds. Friends felt sorry for Nancy and brought casseroles to her house.

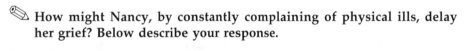 **How might Nancy, by constantly complaining of physical ills, delay her grief? Below describe your response.**

_____

_____

Unfortunately, many grieving people like Nancy unconsciously adopt the "sick person" role in an effort to get their emotional needs met. When people like Nancy take on the sick role, people around them legitimize their very real need to be nurtured and comforted. Nancy may fear that if she expressed her true feelings of grief, people would pull away.

Delayed grief

Sometimes grief is **delayed** for an extended period of time—months or even years. This could occur because the person has an overload of pressing responsibilities, or perhaps the grieving person feels he just can't deal with the grief at the time. When grief is delayed, some other loss—even a very small one—may trigger its release, and it may occur like an avalanche.

The grief-delayer believes that if you postpone expressing grief, it will go away. Obviously it does not. The grief builds and typically emerges in a way that is not good for the mourner.

Delayers may believe that if the grief doesn't vanish, at least at some point they will feel safer in experiencing the pain. Unaware that healing occurs through expression, they continue to postpone. The grief builds up inside and pushes toward the point of explosion. This makes them feel even less capable of experiencing feelings related to the loss.

Conflicted grief

Some people experience **conflicted grief**, in which they exaggerate some of the characteristics of normal grief while they suppress other aspects that also should be present. Sometimes in grieving over a loved one, this reaction occurs because of having had either a dependent or ambivalent relationship with the person. For example, a daughter of a drug-addicted father might exhibit many outward signs of grief at her father's passing yet would suppress her grief about the years of pain his behavior caused her.

Displaced grief

Some people have **displaced grief**. The displacer is the person who takes the expression of grief away from the actual loss and channels the feelings in other directions. For example, Sally did not acknowledge her grief over the loss of her home in a fire but constantly complained of difficulty getting along with her boss. Fred told people, "Everything's fine" when they asked him if he was sad that the last of his three children had gone off to college, yet Fred seemed chronically irritated and upset about even the most minor event. Sally and Fred were not aware that they were displacing their grief.

Some individuals who are displacers become bitter about life in general. Others displace the bitter, unconscious expression of their grief inward and become full of self-hate. They experience crippling depression. At times, these people displace their grief in interactions with other people; at other times they believe people dislike them. Then once again they project unhappiness from within themselves to others.

Displacing grief shifts grief away from its source and on to a less-threatening situation. Personal relationships often become stressed and strained for the displacer, who is unable to acknowledge that he or she is avoiding grief.

✎ **Have you ever experienced any of the five types of unresolved grief mentioned in this lesson? Below put a check by the type you've experienced, and then describe how this occurred in your life.**

❑ Absent grief
❑ Inhibited grief   ❑ Conflicted grief
❑ Delayed grief   ❑ Displaced grief

_____

_____

_____

_____

🌱 **Stop and pray. If you've ever experienced any of these types of unresolved grief, ask God for the courage to help you set these aside and to move into patterns of grief that will help you toward healing.**

Unresolved Grief, Part 2

In day 1 we studied five types of unresolved grief. In today's lesson we'll continue with three more types of unresolved grief that keep people from a normal pattern of healing—chronic, unanticipated, and abbreviated grief.

In **chronic grief**, a person continues to show grief responses that were appropriate in the early stages of grief but that are unhealthy when they remain past those early stages. Mourning continues, but it does not proceed to any sign of closure. The person appears to keep the loss alive with grief. This is especially common in the loss of a person, when the relationship was very intense and had a great deal of emotional investment.

When a loss occurs within a family, it creates a major crisis. The family has functioned according to certain routines. Each person has his or her role, and these roles are crucial to the organization and functioning of the family unit. In a family Mom may be the family budgeter and long-range planner while Dad is the organizer and detail person. In an extended family one sibling may be the keeper of the genealogy while another sibling is the primary caregiver to an elderly parent.

When a family member dies or leaves, an enormous vacuum occurs within the family. The balance is disrupted. Not only does it affect roles; it also affects each person's identity as well. The loss forces each person to make some significant adjustments in his or her own role and the way he or she responds to the other family members.

The family must hammer out new roles for each person, but before that can occur, all need time and space to understand and deal with the loss in their own way. One person might withdraw too much and become isolated unless someone brings him or her back. Out of fear, another may smother the others with love and protection. People will have to feel their way along until the family learns to function once again as a unit.

Unanticipated grief

Unanticipated grief is another classification of unresolved grief. A sudden, unanticipated loss occurs that leaves a person devastated. This might be a sudden job loss or a rapid move as well as an unexpected death or relationship break-up. The loss is such a shock that the person cannot grasp the totality of what has happened.

In her book *Helping People Through Grief*, Delores Kuenning writes: "The impact of sudden death is devastating, for it happens without warning or a chance to anticipate what lies ahead. It allows no time for goodbyes, no time to make amends or ask forgiveness for harsh words spoken in trivial quarrels, and no time to express the love one feels but doesn't verbalize. The unfinished business of the day can never be transacted—it remains unresolved. It is like an unfinished song, the melody stopped in mid-phrase that longs for completion."[1]

In *Grief Counseling and Grief Therapy*, the author identifies seven special features that tend to complicate the grief process for survivors of a sudden-death experience. Although these features mention sudden death, they apply to any type of sudden loss.

1. Sudden death usually leaves the survivor with a sense of unreality that may last a long time.
2. Sudden death fosters a stronger-than-normal sense of guilt expressed in "if only…" statements.
3. In sudden death, the need to blame someone for what happened is extremely strong.
4. Sudden death often involves medical and legal authorities.
5. Sudden death often elicits a sense of helplessness on the part of the survivor.
6. Sudden death leaves the survivor with many regrets and a sense of unfinished business.
7. In the event of a sudden death, there is the need to understand why it happened. Along with this is the need to ascribe not only the cause but the blame. Sometimes God is the only available target, and it is not uncommon to hear someone say, "I hate God."[2]

When you lose someone suddenly, memories of the last time you were together are significant.

Whenever a close loved one dies unexpectedly, the last time you were together is very significant. You remember the last conversation, the last touch, and the surroundings. It stands out vividly—as though somebody hit the "freeze" button on the videocassette player, and the movie of your life froze at this encounter. You tend to play it over and over in your mind.

If your last memory was pleasant, the grieving is easier. That good memory helps to comfort you. But it doesn't always happen that way. You may have wanted to be with the person when he or she died, but the suddenness of the event robbed you of that opportunity. You may have wanted to say more to the person the last time you were together. Or your last encounter could have been an unpleasant conflict, and the relationship had not been fully restored yet. You have a feeling of unfinished business.

Haunted by memories

Sometimes these last unpleasant scenes tend to haunt. Your task then is to soften the memories and images that hurt you so much. You can revise these scenes by editing out the hurtful ones—choosing to go back a bit further in time and dwelling on a scene that better represents your relationship. This scene can comfort you since it better reflects how you felt about the person.

✎ **Describe the last memory you have of the most recent loss in your life.**

_____

_____

Describe how that memory has affected you.

_____

_____

Do you need to do some editing of that memory in order to bring comfort to your life and make your healing occur more easily?
❑ Yes   ❑ No   **If so, to what scene will you return?**

_____

_____

Abbreviated grief

Abbreviated grief is a normal grief response which is not allowed to proceed to resolution. Sometimes people abbreviate their grieving by replacing the loss. A replacer takes the emotions he or she invested in the relationship that ended with loss and prematurely reinvests the feelings in another relationship. The couple conceives a child immediately without grieving for the child they lost; a divorced person remarries too rapidly without recovering from the end of the first marriage; a person replaces too immediately a lost friendship without examining why the first one went awry. The replacement efforts are really a means—usually unconscious—of avoiding facing and resolving grief.

Outsiders sometimes assume that replacers must not have loved the ones they lost because they quickly become involved in new relationships. Actually, often replacers loved very deeply but they try to avoid confronting the feelings related to their losses. They use replacement to avoid the pain. People can replace not only with a person but also by excesses in other areas, such as overwork or plunging frantically into hobbies.

Symptoms of Unresolved Grief

The three primary traits of unresolved grief are (1) absence of a normal grief reaction; (2) a reaction that lingers; or (3) a distortion of a normal grief reaction. When you have one or more of these symptoms, and they continue beyond six months or a year, you may have unresolved grief. The likelihood of unresolved grief increases as the number of symptoms increases.

✎ **The following list contains 16 symptoms of unresolved grief. Place a check mark in the boxes beside the descriptions that you have experienced at some time in your grief process. Underline any symptoms you continue to experience now.**

❏ 1. A pattern of depression that lingers. Guilt and lowered self-esteem often accompany it.

❏ 2. A history of extended or prolonged grief that reflects an already existing difficulty with grief.

❏ 3. A wide variety of symptoms such as guilt, self-blame, panic attacks, feelings of choking, and fears.

❏ 4. Physical symptoms similar to those of the deceased person's terminal illness because of overidentification with the individual.

❏ 5. A restless searching for what was lost with a lot of purposeless, random behavior, and moving about.

❏ 6. Recurring depression that is triggered on specific dates such as anniversaries of the loss, birthday of a deceased person, holidays, and even becoming the same age as the person who died. When these reactions are more extreme than normal responses, unresolved grief can be present.

❏ 7. Feelings that the loss occurred yesterday, even though months or years have passed.

❏ 8. Enshrinement or unwillingness to remove the belongings of a deceased person after a reasonable period of time.

❏ 9. Changes in personal relationships with other significant people after the death.

❏ 10. Withdrawal from normal religious activities and the avoidance of usual mourning activities that are part of the person's culture.

☐ 11. Inability to talk about the loss without breaking down, especially when it occurred over a year before.

☐ 12. Extensive thinking about and noticing themes of loss in life.

☐ 13. Minor losses triggering major grief reactions.

☐ 14. Phobias about death or illness.

☐ 15. Excluding anything or anyone who used to be associated with a significant loss or deceased person.

☐ 16. A compulsion to imitate the deceased person because of overidentification with him or her.[3]

✎ **Below describe how the symptom(s) you marked affect you.**

_____

_____

✎ **Begin to memorize this week's memory verse, Romans 8:26. In the margin write how this verse would comfort you if you experienced any of the types of unresolved grief discussed in day 1 and day 2.**

🐦 **Stop and pray. Ask God to help you recognize symptoms of unresolved grief.**

<table>
<tr><td>

DAY

3

Today's Objective:
You will discover eight reasons for unresolved grief.

Too many losses experienced within a short time can cause overload.

</td><td>

Reasons for Unresolved Grief

Why do some people move through grief so easily while others have such struggles? Can we identify some common clues? Numerous factors predispose a person to difficulty in resolving grief over a loss. We have to allow for variation of responses in grief, but for now we are considering recognizable unresolved grief.

✎ **A list of reasons people fail to resolve their grief appears below. Do any of these reasons apply to you? Put a check in the the box by any that relate to you.**

☐ We cannot deal with the emotional pain of grief, so we tend to resist the process.

☐ We have an excessive need to maintain interaction with the person who no longer is there due to divorce, death, or friendship loss.

☐ We may have excessive guilt that blocks grief. Sometimes we have guilt about behaviors, feelings, or even neglect that occurred in the relationship or situation. If we have very high standards about our interpersonal relationships, we feel guilty easily. This in turn blocks our grieving, since we feel unable to confront our guilt.

☐ We may have excessive dependence on the lost person, so we avoid grieving. We may make statements like, "My life is a total loss without her. I feel like half a person. I cannot function without her." We may try to avoid the reality of the loss because our own personhood seems to be a part of the loss.

☐ Our overload may be another reason for unresolved grief. We can experience a number of losses in a short period of time, and this

</td></tr>
</table>

overload is too much to bear at one time. If we lose several members of our family or even several friends at one time, not only does it produce overload but we also have lost some of the people who in grief could have given support.

❑ Lack of an adequately developed individual identity can lead to unresolved grief. If we haven't matured sufficiently psychologically and emotionally, when a loss confronts us, we tend to regress.

❑ We may fail to grieve because of misbeliefs we hold on to. We fear losing control, for someone has taught us that losing control isn't proper. We do not want to appear weak. We may not want to give up our personal pain because it ties us closer to the person we lost.

❑ Some factors in society actually hinder the grieving process. Numerous losses occur which either are not recognized as losses or which we don't give the significance they deserve. The loss of a pet may not seem significant to friends or relatives of the person who incurred the loss, so they don't participate in or support the loss.

Numerous losses occur which we don't give the significance they deserve.

Several years ago, a friend of mine had to have his 14-year-old cat put to sleep, and he asked me to accompany him. He knew it would be traumatic, and he requested my presence to assist him in his grief and to give support. However, not everyone has support when a pet dies.

A miscarriage is the death of a child just as much as is the death of a 10-year-old. But many times people give insufficient time and attention to a miscarriage situation. Making an adoption plan for a child you are expecting or finding out you can't have children born to you are losses. More and more people report that they experience deep loss after an abortion, and groups are forming to help people with post-abortion syndrome.

✎ **Below describe how those symptoms you marked have affected you.**

_____

_____

❧ **Stop and pray the prayer that appears in the margin.**

Lord,
I've allowed something unhealthy to keep me from resolving my grief appropriately. Just admitting this takes courage. Help me to have continued courage to overcome this.

DAY 4

Today's Objective:
You will identify four more reasons that unresolved grief can occur.

More Reasons

In day 3 we discussed eight reasons for unresolved grief. Today we will identify four more—unacceptable losses, isolation, failure to teach people how to grieve, and uncertainty over the loss.

Some losses seem to be **repulsive** or basically **unacceptable**. Friends, relatives, and others don't want to acknowledge them, let alone assist in the grieving process. Part of their struggle is, "What do I say at a time like this?' What happens when a loved one dies of a cocaine overdose, takes her own life, is murdered by the husband of the woman with whom he was involved, is imprisoned for embezzling funds from an employer, or is arrested for selling drugs? How do people respond today when a loved one dies of AIDS? Do friends and family members lend the support that the grieving persons need? Feelings of distaste and disgust often block a person's ability to grieve or help others in the process.

Isolation

Sometimes people are simply **isolated** and lack other people to help them with the grieving process. Geographical distance could keep the process from occurring. For example, a son of missionary parents was in the States at boarding school. The day he left on a five-day trip to see his parents on the mission field, his father died. By the time he arrived, the remaining family members had comforted one another and had passed through the shock phase. Also, his father had to be buried immediately because of the lack of mortuary facilities. So the son missed the funeral as well.

Failure to teach grieving skills

Another reason for unresolved grief is our **failure to teach people how to deal with loss.** We do not develop good grief skills. Our society has a denial mentality toward loss, and this attitude breeds its own set of problems. For example, when a family member, such as a father dies, often one of the children assumes the role of the "strong one" and takes on the responsibility for all of the arrangements and details. Family members also expect this person to support and encourage the others and let them lean on him or her. This doesn't allow the person the opportunity to conduct his own grief work.

In our society, we give more support to widows than to widowers. But men often have more difficulty than women do in adjusting to the loss of a spouse. Many times people—both male and female—have difficulty adjusting to loss while they try to meet certain roles that accompany their jobs.

Ike Reighard found that trying to keep his chin up for the sake of his congregation became an impossible task after the death of his wife Cindy. He wrote: "I was desperately trying to be a good pastor. I knew others in my congregation were dealing with loss, just as I was. They were down, and the last thing they needed to see was their pastor falling apart. More than anything, I wanted to show them that God helps us through our sorrow. Despite all my efforts to be strong, at times I sat at my desk, and cried like a baby.... Trying to keep my suffering to myself and appear to have more endurance than I had became a heavy load to carry. It eventually locked me in a deadly hold from which I could not free myself. It humiliated me to admit that I was scared—I was a grown man, a minister of the gospel yet—but it was true. I was scared to death!"[4]

Uncertainty over the loss

Effective grieving is difficult when **uncertainty over the loss** occurs. What do you do when a car or family heirloom is stolen, or when a son is missing in action, or when a father's boat is found on a lake after a storm, but he is not to be found? Perhaps you have wondered why people have searched for years for the MIAs from Vietnam or worked to have a soldier's body returned from a grave in North Vietnam, or why people spend days attempting to recover a body from a boating accident or a cave-in. One of the many reasons death needs to be confirmed is so the survivors can grieve the loss.

A time when I couldn't find the words—

_____

_____

_____

✏ **Continue your memory work on this week's Scripture, Romans 8:26. In the margin describe a time when you've been unable to grieve effectively because your sorrow kept the words from forming in your mouth.**

🐛 **Stop and pray. Ask God to send His Spirit to speak for you when you know you should face grief directly but can't find the words to begin.**

Today's Objective:
You will learn 11 steps to take when you are stuck in your grief.

Help for People Who Are Stuck

What can you do when you are stuck in your grief? Perhaps the following suggestions will help because they will give you a sense of being in control of the situation. At least you can see yourself doing something about the problem. Unit 6 on recovery will give you some additional steps to follow.

1. **Identify the issue that does not make sense about your loss.** Perhaps it is a vague question about life or about God's purpose for us. Or it could be a specific question: "Why did this have to happen to me now, at this crucial point in my life?" Ask yourself, "What is bothering me the most?" For several days keep a card with you to record your thoughts as they emerge.

2. **Identify the emotions you feel each day.** Are you experiencing sadness, anger, regret, "if onlys," hurt, or guilt? At what are the feelings directed? Has the intensity of the feelings decreased or increased during the past few days? If your feelings are vague, identifying and labeling them will diminish their power over you. Practice this right now. In the margin box list a few of the feelings you have experienced during the past 24 hours.

3. **State the steps or actions you can take to help you move ahead and to overcome your loss.** Identify what you have done in the past that has helped, or ask a trusted friend to help you view this objectively.

✎ **Below describe some things you have done in the past to help you get over a period of loss or despair.**

_____

_____

How do you envision using this skill to help you over this loss?

_____

_____

Tina answered these questions this way: "In the past I've kept a diary to record my progress. Reading back over the diary helps me see how far I've progressed. I can see how keeping my diary to record my feelings about the loss of my father will help me work through my loss."

4. **Share your loss and grief with others who can listen and support you during this time.** Don't seek out advice-givers, but seek those who are empathetic and can deal with your feelings. Your journey through grief never will be exactly like that of another person; each of us is unique.

5. **Find a person who has experienced a similar loss.** Groups and organizations, such as this support group, abound for losses of all types. Reading books or stories about those who have survived similar experiences can help. If you have been in a group with mixed types of experiences, you may want to go through this support group again—this time with people who have sustained your same type of loss.

Feelings I've had—

_____

_____

_____

_____

He took Peter and the two sons of Zebedee along with him, and he began to be sorrowful and troubled. Then he said to them, "My soul is overwhelmed with sorrow to the point of death. Stay here and keep watch with me."

–Matthew 26:37-38

Set goals for yourself

✎ In the margin box write the names or initials of people who come to mind as having experienced your same type of loss.

6. **Identify the positive characteristics and strengths of your life that have helped you before.** Which of these will help you at this time in your life?

✎ Below is a list of positive character traits. Circle those that you have that can help you again, or add others that the list may not include.

organized	loyal	thorough
generous	insightful	persistent
like to help others	intuitive	tenacious
express emotions well	open, direct	Other _____
meticulous	confident	_____

7. **Spend time reading the Scriptures.** Many Psalms reflect the struggle of human loss and give the comfort and assurance of God's mercies. Some good Psalms for people who hurt include Psalms 6, 10, 18, 22, 25, 31, 34, 38, 42, 57, 69, 73, 77, 86, 88, 103, 116, 121, 139, 143, and 145.

Also, consider Jesus' example. In the verse appearing at left, we see what Jesus did when He approached His death and when He went to pray in the garden of Gethsemane. Not only did Jesus feel sorrowful and troubled, He stated very forthrightly to others how He felt.

8. **When you pray, share your confusion, your feelings, and your hopes with God.** Involve yourself in the worship services of your church since worship is an important element in recovery. You may shed tears at poignant moments in the worship service. Don't be afraid to let the tears fall. They are an important part of your recovery. You can choose not to worry about what people think.

9. **Think about where you want to be in your life two years from now.** Write out some of your dreams and goals. Just setting some goals may encourage you to realize you will recover.

✎ Start on your goal list right now. Below begin writing out a two-year plan for your life. What do you wish your list to be like? What will you accomplish? In what ways will you be growing?

_____

_____

_____

_____

_____

_____

10. **Become familiar with the process of grief.** This book outlines what you may experience and when. If you know what to expect, what you are experiencing won't throw you.

11. **Remember that understanding your grief intellectually is not sufficient.** It can't replace the emotional experience of living through this difficult time. Be patient and allow your feelings to catch up with your mind. Expect mood swings. You can even write notes that say, "Expect mood swings!" and place these notes in obvious places to remind yourself that this behavior is normal.

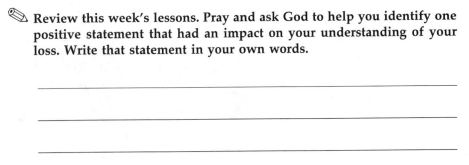 **Stop and pray.** Do as step 8 suggests and share your confusion, your feelings, and your hopes with God. Ask Him to give you courage to act on one or more of these 11 steps that will help you to work through your grief process.

Weekly Work

Review this week's lessons. Pray and ask God to help you identify one positive statement that had an impact on your understanding of your loss. Write that statement in your own words.

_____

_____

_____

Notes

[1]Delores Kuenning, *Helping People Through Grief* (Minneapolis: Bethany House Publishers, 1987), 191.

[2]William Wordon, Grief Counseling and Grief Therapy (New York: Springer Publishing Co. Inc., 1991), p. 84-85. Used by permission.

[3]Therese A. Rando, *Grief, Dying, and Death: Clinical Interventions for Caregivers* (Champaign, Illinois: Research Press, 1984), 63, 64, adapted.

[4]Dwight "Ike" Reighard, *Treasures from the Dark* (Nashville: Thomas Nelson Publishers, 1990), 85.

Learning to Say Goodbye

Case in point

FACING MAJOR CHANGES

During a downsizing at her company, Anne lost her job as an accountant. Her job loss caused her to take a new look at her talents. As a result, she changed to a profession that was better suited for her.

Carl and his wife lost their first child to leukemia. Carl believed that the loss of his child prompted him and his wife to move to a smaller house to simplify their lives so they could spend more time together.

Anne and Carl faced the reality that saying goodbye to something or someone significant in their lives brought about major changes. How did facing reality in this way help them progress through their grief in a healthy manner? In this unit you'll learn more about how you can deal with and benefit from loss.

What you'll learn

This week you will
- describe how changing your relationship with the person or thing you lost will speed your healing;
- make a relationship graph to help you face the reality of your loss;
- decide what to retain and what to give up from your relationship with the thing or person you lost;.
- determine why saying goodbye to the person or thing you lost is necessary;
- write a goodbye letter to the person or thing you lost.

What you'll study

Facing the Changes	Relating to What You Lost	Reinvesting Your Energies	The Importance of Goodbyes	How to Say Goodbye
DAY 1	DAY 2	DAY 3	DAY 4	DAY 5

Memory verse

This week's verse of Scripture to memorize
Therefore, if anyone is in Christ, he is a new creation; the old has gone, the new has come!

—2 Corinthians 5:17

Facing the Changes

Today's Objective:
You will describe how changing your relationship with the person or thing you lost will speed your healing.

Besides experiencing the pain of loss, you also must adjust to the void the person, object, or relationship that is gone leaves. Whether your loss was a dream, a job, a friend, a pet, a child, a spouse, a parent, or a dating relationship, an empty place exists in your life. You must become accustomed to the absence of something that was a very important part of your life. Your task now is to learn how to function without whatever is gone.

If your loss was a person, you learn to move on without that relationship. Even when a close friend moves away, this kind of adjustment is necessary. You automatically go to the phone to give her a call, or you walk down the block to drop in, and then you realize the person no longer is there. A widow turns over in bed to put her arm around her husband, and the reality that he no longer is a part of her life hits her.

In the loss of a person, you have to learn how to function without interaction and validation from that person. The lack of the person's physical presence in your life means your needs, hopes, dreams, expectations, feelings, and thoughts will change. Slowly over time, the reality of separation begins to sink in. You realize, "For now, I exist without this person as a part of my life."

When did it hit?

✎ **How has this happened for you? Below describe a point at which the stark reality of your loss seemed to "hit" the strongest?**

_____

_____

_____

_____

Even as I write these words, I still feel the freshness of my son's death. We purchased a pumpkin for Halloween, but Matthew won't be here to sit on it or to have his picture taken with it. He won't be coming home for the Thanksgiving or Christmas holidays either. When those days arrive, we will feel the lack of his presence. We must experience and accept it.

Whatever loss you experienced, you will make changes. Not being able to continue in school may mean major changes in your time, future hopes, economic state, other people's expectations of you, and your feelings about yourself. If you lost a person, the loss of companionship, how much you depend-

Many reminders

ed on the person, his or her opinions—all of these are new and separate losses that make up the major loss in your life.

Each time you start to respond to the person who no longer is there, you discover your loss again. It is a fact, and you will have many reminders. Even when a business relationship dissolves, you automatically may turn to the person to take care of a task that person usually deals with for you—only to realize that the person is gone.

✎ In Unit 2 you identified some of the roles that the person you have lost played in your life. Since that time have you identified any additional roles? If so describe them below.

_____

_____

_____

Whenever you lose a significant person or situation, you have to broaden your roles and your skills and learn to function without what you lost. You change what you do, take over responsibility, or find another person to help. Some things you simply won't do anymore. Adjustment means not behaving the same way you did when the person or thing was a part of your world.

Never quite the same

For many people, a loss means acquiring a new identity. You never will be quite the same as you were before the loss. As one person said, "That portion of my life is history. I never will be that way or be that person again." Look at the people around you and think about how their losses were turning points in their lives. Often people point to the time of loss as a turn in the road for the direction of their lives. My mother lost her first husband when she was 34. When she was 61, her second husband (my father) died in an automobile accident. Major changes occurred after each of these events.

✎ What about you? Describe what changes you already see occurring as a result of your loss. If your loss is too recent or you haven't yet identified any change, then think about someone else whose loss was a turning point in his or her life, and describe the change you observed.

_____

_____

_____

_____

_____

Anne wrote that her job loss caused her to take a new look at her talents. As a result, she changed to a profession that was better suited for her. Carl said that the loss of their child prompted him and his wife to move to a smaller house to simplify their lives so they could spend more time together.

When Jesus saw his mother there, and the disciple whom he loved standing nearby, he said to his mother, "Dear woman, here is your son," and to the disciple, "Here is your mother." From that time on, this disciple took her into his home.

–John 19:26-27

When Jesus was hanging on the cross, He already was anticipating the change that would occur in the life of His mother, Mary. Even as He was dying, He began helping her make that change. He no longer would be there to fulfill the role of son in her life. He summoned John to help her with that transition. See the Scripture appearing at left.

❤ Stop and pray. Ask God to help you use whatever change your loss has brought about to make your life more Christ-honoring.

Relating to What You Lost

Today's Objective:
You will make a relationship graph to help yourself face the reality of your loss.

Perhaps your most crucial task is to develop a new relationship with what you lost. This change of relationship involves several steps. For the purposes of this discussion, we will consider death or divorce as the loss, although these steps can apply to any loss.

The change involves keeping the loved one alive in your memory in a healthy and appropriate manner and forming a new identity without this person's physical presence in your life. As you complete your grief work, the emotional energy that you once invested in the person you lost now is freed to be reinvested in other people, activities, and hopes that in turn can give you emotional satisfaction.

In divorce, courts work out a new relationship with the one lost. But what do you do about a spouse or child you lost through death? Death ends the person's life but not your relationship. This is not morbid or pathological. It is a very normal response. If people tell you that the best way to deal with your loss is to forget the person, they inhibit your grief experience.

Keeping people alive

We keep people alive all the time as we reflect on their achievement and on their impact. We hear people say, "I wonder what he would think if he were alive today," or "Wouldn't she be surprised to see all of this?"

✎ **You may have made statements similar to these about the loved one or relationship you lost. If so, describe below.**

_____

_____

_____

_____

Thinking about what a loved one might have done or said is normal. What is abnormal is the feeling that you must do or see things just the way the lost loved one did. Sometimes in divorce, a spouse continues to allow the memory of a pressuring spouse to dominate his or her present life. This is unhealthy. A statement such as, "She would have wanted me to paint the house this color," could indicate a continued, unhealthy emotional investment.

Distorted memories

Sometimes when we lose something that has played a significant part in our lives, our memory of it becomes distorted. We sometimes recall only the positive aspects. But in time, we can review thoughts and memories realistically to include good and bad, positive and negative, situations we are glad occurred, and those we wish had not happened. By doing this, a balanced, realistic, accurate pool of memories develops. This is the image that you need to develop the new relationship with the person.

You may benefit by making a relationship history graph about the person you lost and identifying the positive and negatives of your relationship. On the following page is one such graph.

A relationship graph

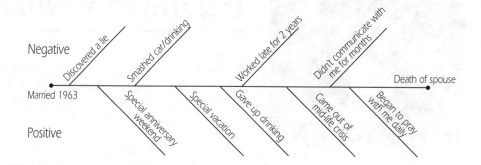

Negative

Discovered a lie

Smashed car/drinking

Worked late for 2 years

Didn't communicate with me for months

Death of spouse

Married 1963

Positive

Special anniversary weekend

Special vacation

Gave up drinking

Came out of mid-life crisis

Began to pray with me daily

On the bottom portion of the graph, we've listed positive events and experiences. You would benefit from listing five to 15 separate events. The length of the vertical line indicates how much it meant to you. On the top part of the line, identify negative, upsetting, or hurtful experiences. Again, the length of the vertical line indicates the intensity of the experience.

In the space below draw your own graph. We've provided the vertical line. You can add the lines extending from it.

As you complete this you may find that other significant events come to mind. Add them. On a separate sheet of paper write a paragraph describing each event, both positive and negative, as completely as possible. Allow your feelings to emerge. Some of them may occur under the category of regrets or "if onlys." Your list may look like this:

- My feelings are all mixed up. I wish they were more clear.
- I'll never forget the times we prayed together. They meant so much.
- I'm glad we have pictures and a video from our anniversaries.
- I'm still hurt about the drinking. I wish it hadn't been part of our marriage.
- I'm sorry for my angry outbursts.
- I'm angry you died so young. I feel cheated. Our marriage was getting better when you died. We needed more time.
- I wish we could have talked more. I wanted to tell you so much.

Some of these statements may bring to mind such thoughts as: *I wish things could have been different. I wish things could have been better. I wish we had spent more time together. I wonder what would have happened if....* These statements reflect our own critical attitude toward what we did or didn't do and what the lost person did or didn't do. If we remain in this critical stage, inaccurate memories of the relationship begin to emerge. The more this occurs, the more difficulty we have completing our grief work. If we are too critical of ourselves, we tend to overcompliment the person no longer there.

If we are too critical of ourselves, we tend to overcompliment the person no longer there.

✎ As you reflect on the "if onlys," regrets, and what you wanted better or different or more of, what do you discover about your relationship? What events still need to be resolved?

_____

_____

_____

Do you keep reliving your experience of loss? Then do you wonder if remembering is necessary or normal? It is both. Repetitious reviewing helps you fully realize the fact of your loss. Each time you review your loss and the surrounding events, your understanding of it will increase. You may hesitate because the memories are painful, but the more you review them, the more reality sets in, and the more control you have over your recovery.

✎ Begin to memorize this week's memory verse, 2 Corinthians 5:17. In the margin write it three times.

🌱 Stop and pray. Ask God to help you to face the reality that life has changed for you in a big way. Ask Him to help you cope with change.

DAY 3

Today's Objective:
You will decide what to retain and what to give up from your relationship with the thing or person you lost.

A time when I didn't believe I could go on—

_____

_____

_____

_____

Reinvesting Your Energies

Some people never seem to surrender what they have lost. They hang on and dwell on what they never had or what they lost, and it dominates their lives. Often, they become bitter. When a child dies, some parents become involved in enshrinement. They keep their child alive by keeping his room just the way it was when he was alive. Unfortunately, this prolongs grief.

Some respond with just the opposite reaction. After the loss occurs, they act as though the situation never existed. Neither of these are healthy responses. People need to achieve a balance.

We can "hold on" in a healthy way to something we lost. When you lose a parent, a spouse, a child, or a job, you don't want to forget that the person or situation once existed. In healthy remembrance, you find yourself thinking, doing, saying, and feeling things that show the other person or situation continues to influence you.

One healthy way to properly relate to a deceased loved one is to recognize that the other person is gone and that you are still alive. At first you may not feel as though you are alive. Sometimes people say they cannot or do not want to go on without the one who left or died.

✎ Have you said you cannot go on? Have you had times in which you felt more dead than alive? In the margin box describe one such time.

Although such times are normal, the time also arrives when you emotionally let go and reinvest in life in a new way.

Another step is deciding what existed about your life with the other person and your life together that you can and should retain. It means deciding what would be healthy. Do you continue to—
- go to the same coffee shop each morning for breakfast?
- go on an evening walk around the park?
- maintain any of the daily or weekly routines the two of you shared?

✎ **Below describe your own situation. What activities from your former situation have you decided to keep and which ones have you decided to give up after your loss?**

I continue to... _____

_____

I have discontinued... _____

_____

Healthy ways to relate

You can choose some healthy ways to relate to the memory of those you have lost through death. Depending on the circumstances and relationship, you might choose to—
- learn more about their favorite activities and involvements;
- look at home movies or videos, listen to tapes of them, or reflect on some of their stories to bring back memories of them;
- try some of their favorite foods or engage in their former activities, just to experience what they did.

People preserve memories by visiting the deceased person's childhood school, job, and by visiting the cemetery. Years after my father died, I located his original homestead in Woolich, Maine, and even found some distant relatives. This brought back memories and expanded my knowledge of my dad. Part of who you are today and how you respond today is based on your relationship with that person, so doing things based on what you learned about the person, or reflecting on memories is normal.

In the loss of a spouse, a person experiences an identity change from "we" to "I." This can be one of the most painful transitions of all. Some of your friendships may change as well. You will retain old friendships, but you will make adjustments. Your identity may have been as a couple, and most of your friendships were couple relationships. But now you are alone. Your time with couples will diminish. You will need both old and new relationships with people who share portions of your new identity. If your job situation changes, some of your friendships may change as well. In your former hometown you may have been the PTA president or the chairman of deacons at your church. A relocation changes this. No matter what you lost, you benefit from being with and identifying with others who have experienced the same loss as you.

You will need both old and new relationships with people who share portions of your new identity.

❧ **Stop and pray. Thank God for those persons who already have helped you in your new identity adjustment. In the margin write their initials.**

Recovery involves reinvesting your emotional energy in something new that can give you satisfaction and fulfillment. The relationship with the person or object you lost cannot do this anymore, but I am not talking about a replacement. A new cat cannot replace the old one, a new person is not a replacement for a former love, and any attempt to make them replicas is an unhealthy response. Instead of replacing, you can reinvest in a service organization, a ministry, a new career, or a new hope.

 What progress have you made in this area? Have you begun to reinvest your emotional energies in some new way? Or are you considering some new goals and dreams for the future? Below describe steps you've taken in this direction.

_____

_____

 Continue to memorize this week's memory verse, 2 Corinthians 5:17. Refresh your memory by referring to page 62 if necessary. In the margin describe how this verse might help you if you are trying to prepare for the new life ahead of you as you recover from your loss.

The pile plan

A major adjustment for anyone who has lost a loved one in death is what to do with the items left behind. This could involve tools, toys, clothes, specialty books, and other things. One way of dealing with this is the pile plan. Sometimes a family member or close friend can help. Take all the items and make three piles. In one pile place items you are sure you want to keep. In the next one put those you know you want to dispose of. The third pile contains the things you are just not certain what to do about. Put away the items you want, give the others away, and place the uncertain items in boxes and keep them for a while until you are sure of a plan for them. This is not an easy task. It is not without pain. But our lives do go on—different and new. How different and new depends on our grief work.

DAY 4

Today's Objective:
You will determine why saying goodbye to the person or thing you lost is necessary.

The Importance of Goodbyes

Retirement parties and farewell luncheons are opportunities to share goodbyes. When a friend leaves, loved ones go home after a visit, or a co-worker retires, our goodbyes have sadness in them. With every loss we need to recognize that a connection is broken and that life will be different. In death the funeral service is a recognition that a person is gone. It provides an opportunity for the mourners to say goodbye. At the funeral of my father, who was killed in an automobile accident when I was 22, one of his close friends put his hand on the casket and said, "Goodbye, Harry." For recovery to occur, we need to look back and say goodbye.

Sometimes we feel a lingering sadness because others failed to say goodbye in a proper way. Some events that contribute to incomplete feelings are—
- not enough friends or fellow workers respond with written expression, or they were unwilling to talk about the loss;
- the plaque or marker at the grave site either was delayed for months or was not appropriate;
- the person conducting the service failed to make the service meaningful because of lack of information;

- very few people arrived to pay their respects at the funeral home or at the actual service;
- a lack of recognition for the person retiring or leaving a job;
- a pet that ran away or was stolen, affording no opportunity to say good-bye;
- others downplaying the significance of a loss, making it difficult for the person to properly acknowledge it.

✎ **As you read this list, do you identify with some of these events that have caused you lingering sadness? Put a check mark by any that apply to you, or below, describe what contributed to incomplete feelings.**

_____

_____

When you say goodbye, you acknowledge that you no longer will share your life with whatever you lost. You always will have the memory, but now you acknowledge that you will live without what you lost.

What helps one person through grief may not mean much to others. Some parents who experience miscarriage simply move on with their lives. Others have a memorial service. Women who had abortions years ago often have memorial services to recognize the deaths of their children.

Being able to anticipate a loss makes it easier to cope. Sometimes people exclaim in anger, "He left, and I never got a chance to say goodbye to him." Being able to say goodbye before the loss will help in the grieving process. Just after the doctor told us that our son Matthew probably would die within the hour, we stood at his bedside and said goodbye to him. We have said it more than once since he died. Often we say it when we find one of his personal items or even rediscover a memory.

Being able to say goodbye before the loss will help in the grieving process.

Some people drive to the location of a former place of employment, stand in front of the building, and say goodbye. Sometimes the farewell is out of a storehouse of positive memories and other times out of anger about the severing circumstances.

✎ **Who or what have you said goodbye to in your life? Below identify three things you have said goodbye to in your life. Describe how you said goodbye.**

I said goodbye to—   How I said goodbye—

1. _____   1. _____

   _____   _____

2. _____   2. _____

   _____   _____

3. _____   3. _____

   _____   _____

In reading this material, have you realized something or someone you need to say goodbye to? No matter when the loss occurred, you can say goodbye even now.

I once counseled a man who had not returned to the grave site of his brother since the burial two years before. Not being able fully to grieve for his brother clearly was one of his difficulties. The next day he spent several hours at the grave site. He said goodbye, and at last a chapter in his life was closed.

A way to say goodbye

Writing is a good way to say goodbye to many kinds of losses. A letter is both a way to say goodbye and a way to express intense feelings of loss. It may be an angry letter or one full of joy or sadness. Here are some examples:
- A man wrote a friend dying of cancer and expressed appreciation for him.
- A woman wrote a letter to an elementary school teacher who was retiring. She expressed sadness that the teacher never would teach her children.
- A former addict wrote a farewell letter to his drugs and described what a problem they had been for him.
- Many women have written goodbye letters to one of their breasts before or after a mastectomy. Such letters help the women with a traumatic loss.

Goodbye letters also help during life's major transitions. I encourage parents who are about to see their daughter or son married to write the new son- or daughter-in-law a "welcome to the family" letter as well as a letter to their own son or daughter saying goodbye to him or her as an unmarried child. We did this when our daughter Sheryl married. (You can find this letter in the final chapter of my book *Always Daddy's Girl*.) I call letters like this transitional goodbye letters that also introduce new stages of life.

Saying goodbye is not morbid, pathological, or a sign of being out of control. Saying goodbye is a healthy way to transition into the next phase of life.

✎ **In day 5 we will ask you to write a goodbye letter to the person, thing, or situation that you lost. Based on what you read in this day's material, begin thinking about what you will say in your goodbye letter. In the margin begin jotting down some areas you think you need to cover.**

❦ **Stop and pray, asking God to prepare you to write your goodbye letter.**

DAY 5

Today's Objective:
You will write a goodbye letter to the person or thing you lost.

How to Say Goodbye

How do you say goodbye? First, identify what you think you need to express. How can you express your appreciation and regrets? How can you complete something that never was finished between the two of you or between you and the situation?

Next, write an actual goodbye letter or talk out loud to the person or whatever you have lost. If your letter is to a loved one who died, use the name you used most of the time in your life with this person. You can address a goodbye letter to a lost dream, a lost hope, a business, or even a change in your vocational life. One divorced woman actually wrote a letter to her marriage and addressed it as though the loss were a real person. Indicate that it is a goodbye letter, and then share what you want to say. The more regrets and "if onlys" you have, the more important your letter may be, since this is your opportunity to express what you never verbalized.

Read it aloud

It helps to let your letter rest for a day and then read it aloud to yourself or to a trusted friend. In most situations, this is not a letter that you actually mail to someone. For example, if your loss is a lost friendship, you would not mail the letter to that friend, but the letter would help you identify your feelings.

Recently a woman shared with me the letters she had written to her deceased mother. This process of writing took more than 15 months and included 17 letters. Your *Recovering from the Losses of Life* support group facilitator likely has given you a copy of this letter for you to refer to as an example of how helpful letters of this nature can be.

✎ **Now, based on the information you've read here and in yesterday's work, write your goodbye letter. Use a separate sheet or sheets of paper for your work. You may want to write several letters over a period of time, as described in the previous paragraph. Let your true feelings emerge.**

We have other ways to express goodbyes. Sending a contribution to a church or charity in the name of the person is one way. Some people set up a living and lasting memorial through a scholarship, by donating a painting, planting a flower garden or a tree, or having a plaque made.

A different perspective

When Christians die, for us the experience means having to say goodbye, but for them it is a matter of being able to say hello to their Lord. This is why our feelings sometimes can be a mixture—we are sad for our loss, but we also have a sense of joy for what the deceased person now experiences. We have a void in our lives, but the deceased person's life is now full and complete. The Christian death is a transition—a tunnel leading from this world into the next. As we grieve, the reality of our loss often overshadows the reality of where our loved one is. We need reminders of the meaning of death from the biblical perspective. For the Christian death is a homegoing. David Morley beautifully describes the journey:

"The most glorious anticipation of the Christian is that, at the time of death, he will come face-to-face with his blessed Lord, his wonderful, patient Redeemer, who all of those years continued to love him in spite of the countless times the man ignored Him and went his willful way. We will not be encountering a stranger, but the best and the most intimate friend that we have ever had. When we think of death as a time of revelation and reunion, we immediately remove its venom. We can say with the Apostle Paul, 'Oh death, where is thy sting? Oh grave, where is thy victory?' (I Corinthians 15:15)"[1]

✎ **Can you allow the hope of heaven to remove the sting of loss you feel? Below write how you feel when you read Paul's words above.**

Then I saw a new heaven and a new earth, for the first heaven and the first earth had passed away, and there was no longer any sea. I saw the Holy City, the new Jerusalem, coming down out of heaven from God, prepared as a bride beautifully dressed for her husband. And I heard a loud voice from the throne saying, "Now the dwelling of God is with men, and he will live with them. They will be his people, and God himself will be with them and be their God. He will wipe every tear from their eyes. There will be no more death or mourning or crying or pain, for the old order of things has passed away.

–Revelation 21:1-5

A Christian is the one person who can have a different perspective on death. A Christian has a guarantee—not just of life here but forever. As one author said: "Death is ugly and it is repulsive, but it is not, I repeat, not able to bring the life of a Christian to a dreadful, screeching halt. God has worked out an alternate plan and it is a plan filled with soaring hope."

In Max Lucado's inspirational book *The Applause of Heaven*, he concludes with a chapter on going home. He begins the chapter by describing his conclusion to a long trip and finally arriving at the airport. His wife and three daughters are excited that he is home. But one of them has a very interesting response. In the midst of the shouts of joy that he is home, she stops long enough to clap. She applauds for him. Isn't that different? But isn't it affirming and appropriate! Then he proceeds to talk about the Christian's ultimate homegoing. Surely Jesus, too, will clap when we arrive home. In the Scriptures appearing at left we read John's description of what our homegoing will be like.

Every person on earth is appointed to die some time. We fear it, resist it, try to postpone it, and even deny its existence. But it won't work. We cannot keep our loved ones from dying. We cannot keep ourselves from dying. But we can see it from God's perspective. Max Lucado concludes his book with what homegoing means from a new perspective:

"Before you know it, your appointed arrival time will come; you'll descend the ramp and enter the City. You'll see faces that are waiting for you. You'll hear your name spoken by those you love. And, maybe, just maybe—in the back, behind the crowds—the One who would rather die than live without you will remove his pierced hands from his heavenly robe and...applaud."[2]

Yes, your loved ones who died are saying hello. You have said good-bye to them. Soon you will be saying hello to a new day without them—for now!

✎ Say your memory verse aloud three times from memory.

🕊 **Stop and pray, thanking God for His wonderful promise that death has no sting for a Christian. Ask Him to help you tell the Gospel story to others so they can have that promise of eternal life.**

Weekly Work

✎ **Review this week's lessons. Pray and ask God to help you identify one positive statement that had an impact on your understanding of your loss. Write that statement in your own words.**

_____

_____

Notes
[1]David C. Morley, *Halfway Up the Mountain* (Old Tappan, New Jersey: Fleming H. Revell Company, 1979), 77, 78.
[2]Max Lucado, *The Applause of Heaven* (Dallas, Texas: Word Incorporated, 1990), 186 ,187.

Recovering from Loss

> ### THE NEXT STEPS
>
> Anita had gone through a grief-recovery support group. She grew through her relationship with the group members, and she completed her workbook material daily. She benefited from learning that other people had undergone experiences similar to her own. She felt a little bewildered about what she should do next. Her support system would no longer be available to her, and she wondered, "What do I do now?"
>
> This unit provides helps for people like Anita who want to continue their recovery and growth after they complete the six core units of this workbook.

What you'll learn

This week you will
- determine that you can choose to do something constructive with your loss;
- complete a helpful evaluation with which you can measure how you are progressing in your recovery;
- determine how to keep a personal journal that records your progress in your recovery;
- list strengths you have developed because of your loss and evaluate ways you can use these strengths to help others;
- identify the next steps to take after completing the six core units of this study.

What you'll study

Recovering A Matter of Choice	A Helpful Evaluation	Keeping A Journal of Progress	Help Through the Valley	Where Do I Go from Here?
DAY 1	DAY 2	DAY 3	DAY 4	DAY 5

Memory verse

This week's verse of Scripture to memorize
Do not fear, for I am with you; do not be dismayed, for I am your God. I will strengthen you and help you; I will uphold you with my righteous right hand.
—Isaiah 41:10

DAY 1

Today's Objective:
You will learn that you can choose to do something constructive with your loss.

Recovering: A Matter of Choice

"How will I know when I have recovered?" "Will it ever be over?" "Will I ever reach a time when I am through mourning?" "How will I feel when I've recovered from my loss?"

Have you ever asked these common questions? We want to know both when it will happen and how we will know. Recovery is essential for any kind of loss, but the actual recovery period will vary, depending on the type of loss, the intensity of the loss, and our ability to deal with grief.

✎ **Think back to the most recent loss in your life. If you believe you are recovering, describe below how you knew when your recovery work was going to succeed.**

_____

_____

_____

One woman answered that she knew she had begun recovering from her father's death because she no longer shed tears in church when the congregation sang certain hymns. One man answered that he knew he was recovered from the loss of a special friend when he could go to some of their favorite places and do so with a sense of peace in his heart.

Adjusting to the effects

After you undergo surgery, you go to a recovery room, where you stay for a few hours until the effects of the anesthesia begin to wear off. The term recovery is a bit misleading to describe this room. It certainly doesn't mean total recovery. It means helping you adjust to the effects of the operation so you are ready for the real recovery, which will take time.

Ann Kaiser Stearns describes the process of recovery:

"Recovery from loss is like having to get off the main highway every so many miles because the direct route is under reconstruction. The road signs reroute you through little towns you hadn't expected to visit and over bumpy roads you hadn't wanted to bounce around on. You are basically traveling in the appropriate direction. On the map, however, the course you are following has the look of shark's teeth instead of a straight line. Although you are gradually getting there, you sometimes doubt that you will ever meet up with the finished highway."[1]

Recovery does not mean a once-and-for-all conclusion to your loss and grief. It means regaining your ability to function as you once did as you resolve and integrate your loss into your life. Recovery means you get your capabilities and attributes back so you can use them. Part of the process means you no longer fight your loss but accept it. Acceptance doesn't mean you would have chosen this situation or that you like it. You have learned to live with it as a part of your life. Recovery doesn't mean you don't mourn occasionally. It means you learn to live with your loss so you can go on with your life.

Recovery means you learn to live with your loss so you can go on with your life.

✎ **According to the paragraphs you just read, which one of the following statements is true about recovery?**

❑ Recovery is a once-and-for-all conclusion to your grief.
❑ Recovery means that you never mourn again.
❑ Recovery means that you learn to like what happened to you.
❑ Recovery means regaining your ability to function and integrating the loss into your life.

Recovery doesn't mean that your grief and mourning are over, nor does it mean that you are happy about your situation. It does mean that you integrate the loss so that you can function and move forward with your life. Only the last statement is true. Recovering means reinvesting in life and looking for new relationships and new dreams. A newfound source of joy is possible. But you may believe that to experience the joys of life again somehow is wrong. Besides, you may think that if you begin to hope or trust again, you could experience another loss.

✎ **What might be causing you difficulty in reinvesting in life at this time?**

_____

_____

_____

Describe what you might do that would help you to participate in life more fully.

_____

_____

One person responded that her feeling that her failure as a mother contributed to her daughter's terminal illness kept her from reinvesting in life. She wrote that visits with a counselor were helping her examine her feelings of overresponsibility and would help her participate in life more fully.

✎ **Read the Psalm appearing in the margin. Underline words and phrases in the Psalm that you believe apply to your grief and recovery.**

You may have underlined such phrases as "you brought me up from the grave," "you hid your face," or "when you favored me." You probably have felt a combination of these things: that in your grief you were going to die, that God had turned away from you, and that at times in your grief, God also was looking out for you.

In recovery you can discover that weeping will not last forever. You may have some clothes of mourning that you would like to exchange for clothes of joy. You can do that! You have a choice. Most people do not have a choice in their loss, but everyone has a choice in recovery. The changes in your identity, relationships, new roles, and even abilities either can be positive or negative. This is where you have a choice. Some people choose to live in denial as though nothing has happened. Some people stay stuck in the early stages of grief and choose to live a life of bitterness and blame. Some become so hardened and angry that people have difficulty being around them. You have the choice of doing something constructive with your loss.

I will exalt you, O Lord, for you lifted me out of the depths and did not let my enemies gloat over me. O Lord my God, I called to you for help and you healed me. O Lord, you brought me up from the grave; you spared me from going down into the pit. Sing to the Lord, you saints of his, praise his holy name. For his anger lasts only a moment, but his favor lasts a lifetime; weeping may remain for a night, but rejoicing comes in the morning. When I felt secure, I said, "I will never be shaken." O Lord, when you favored me, you made my mountain stand firm; but when you hid your face, I was dismayed. To you, O Lord, I called; to the Lord I cried for mercy; What gain is there in my destruction, in my going down into the pit? Will the dust praise you? Will it proclaim your faithfulness? Hear, O Lord, and be merciful to me; O Lord, be my help. You turned my wailing into dancing; you removed my sackcloth and clothed me with joy, that my heart may sing to you and not be silent. O Lord, my God, I will give you thanks forever.

–Psalm 30: 1-12

Stop and pray. Ask God to help you choose to do something constructive with your loss.

A Helpful Evaluation

DAY 2

Today's Objective:
You will complete a helpful evaluation that will show how you are progressing in your recovery.

A helpful evaluation

Does any kind of criteria exist that a person can use to evaluate whether or not recovery is occurring? Yes, it does. Dr. Therese Rando[2] has made an outstanding contribution to the study of grief and recovery. She suggests that you can see recovery by observing changes in yourself, in your relationship with what you lost, and in your relationship with the world and other people in it.

As you complete the following evaluation, the conclusions you reach may help you to decide where you are in your recovery. The scale below is geared toward the loss of a person, but you can adapt it to other losses as well. People often find that going through this evaluation with a person who can assist them with an objective viewpoint is useful.

On a scale of 0 to 10, with 0 meaning "not at all" and 10 meaning "total recovery in that area," rate yourself in response to each question below.

Changes in Myself Because of My Loss

I have returned to my normal levels of functioning in most areas of my life.

    0   1   2   3   4   5   6   7   8   9   10

My overall symptoms of grief have declined.

    0   1   2   3   4   5   6   7   8   9   10

My feelings do not overwhelm me when I think about my loss or when someone mentions it.

    0   1   2   3   4   5   6   7   8   9   10

Most of the time I feel alright about myself.

    0   1   2   3   4   5   6   7   8   9   10

Without feeling guilty, I enjoy myself and what I experience.

    0   1   2   3   4   5   6   7   8   9   10

My anger has diminished, and when it occurs, I deal with it appropriately.

    0   1   2   3   4   5   6   7   8   9   10

I don't avoid thinking about things that could be or are painful.

    0   1   2   3   4   5   6   7   8   9   10

My hurt has diminished and I understand it.

    0   1   2   3   4   5   6   7   8   9   10

I can think about positive things.

    0   1   2   3   4   5   6   7   8   9   10

I have completed doing what I need to do about my loss.

0   1   2   3   4   5   6   7   8   9   10

My pain does not dominate my thoughts or my life.

0   1   2   3   4   5   6   7   8   9   10

I have dealt with the secondary losses that accompanied my major loss.

0   1   2   3   4   5   6   7   8   9   10

I can deal with special days or dates without being totally overwhelmed by memories.

0   1   2   3   4   5   6   7   8   9   10

I can remember the loss on occasion without pain and without crying.

0   1   2   3   4   5   6   7   8   9   10

My life has meaning and significance to it.

0   1   2   3   4   5   6   7   8   9   10

At this time I am able to ask the question "How?" rather than "Why?"

0   1   2   3   4   5   6   7   8   9   10

In spite of my loss, I see hope and purpose in life.

0   1   2   3   4   5   6   7   8   9   10

I have energy and can feel relaxed during the day.

0   1   2   3   4   5   6   7   8   9   10

I no longer fight the fact that the loss has occurred. I have accepted it.

0   1   2   3   4   5   6   7   8   9   10

I am learning to be comfortable with my new identity and in being without what I lost.

0   1   2   3   4   5   6   7   8   9   10

I understand that my feelings about the loss will return periodically, and I can accept that.

0   1   2   3   4   5   6   7   8   9   10

I understand what grief means and have a greater appreciation for it.

0   1   2   3   4   5   6   7   8   9   10

Changes in My Relationship with the Person I Lost

I remember our relationship realistically with positive and negative memories.

0   1   2   3   4   5   6   7   8   9   10

The relationship I have with the person I lost is healthy and appropriate.

0   1   2   3   4   5   6   7   8   9   10

I feel alright about not thinking about the loss for a time. I am not betraying the one I lost.

0   1   2   3   4   5   6   7   8   9   10

I have a new relationship with the person I have lost. I know appropriate ways of keeping the person "alive."

    0   1   2   3   4   5   6   7   8   9   10

I no longer go on a search for my loved one.

    0   1   2   3   4   5   6   7   8   9   10

I don't feel compelled to hang on to the pain.

    0   1   2   3   4   5   6   7   8   9   10

The ways I keep my loved one alive are healthy and acceptable.

    0   1   2   3   4   5   6   7   8   9   10

I can think about things in life other than what I lost.

    0   1   2   3   4   5   6   7   8   9   10

My life has meaning even though this person is gone.

    0   1   2   3   4   5   6   7   8   9   10

Changes I Have Made in Adjusting to My New World

I have integrated my loss into my world and I can relate to others in a healthy way.

    0   1   2   3   4   5   6   7   8   9   10

I can accept the help and support of other people.

    0   1   2   3   4   5   6   7   8   9   10

I am open about my feelings in other relationships.

    0   1   2   3   4   5   6   7   8   9   10

I believe it is alright for life to go on even though my loved one is gone.

    0   1   2   3   4   5   6   7   8   9   10

I have developed an interest in people and things outside myself that have no relationship to the person I lost.

    0   1   2   3   4   5   6   7   8   9   10

I have put the loss in perspective.

    0   1   2   3   4   5   6   7   8   9   10

What did you learn about yourself in the process of taking this evaluation? No right or wrong scores exist for these scales; obviously the more answers at or near 10, the closer you are at being at an ideal state in your recovery. Go back and study those areas in which you scored from 0 to 5. Evaluate what steps you need to take to boost your rating in that area.

✎ **Begin to memorize this week's memory verse, Isaiah 41:10. In the margin write it three times.**

❦ **Stop and pray. Ask God to help you as you process the evaluation you just took. Ask Him to help you in the areas where you still need work, and praise Him for His leading you in the areas where you record the most progress.**

Keeping a Journal of Progress

One of the best ways to identify your progress is by keeping a personal journal. This will show your progress even though your feelings say you are getting nowhere. Your journal is your private property and is not for anyone else to read. It is an expression of what you feel and of your recovery climb. You can write it in any style. It can be simple statements, poems, or prayers that reflect your journey. Your entries may be as brief as a few words or as long as you desire.

Today's Objective:
You will determine how to keep a journal that records the progress you make in recovery.

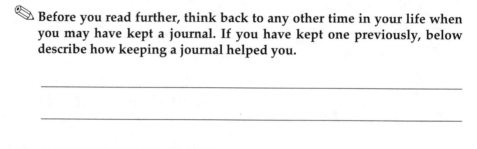 **Before you read further, think back to any other time in your life when you may have kept a journal. If you have kept one previously, below describe how keeping a journal helped you.**

_____

_____

_____

I cried unto the Lord with my voice; with my voice unto the Lord did I make my supplication. I poured out my complaint before him; I shewed before him my trouble. When my spirit was overwhelmed within me, then thou knewest my path. In the way wherein I walked have they privily laid a snare for me... Bring my soul out of prison, that I may praise thy name; the righteous shall compass me about; for thou shalt deal bountifully with me.

–Psalm 142:1-3, 7 KJV

The psalms are filled with examples of this type of process. Consider the verses from Psalm 142 appearing at left. Without mincing words, the writer pours out his soul to the Lord; then later in the Psalm he shows his progress and his confidence in the Lord by stating his belief, "thou shalt deal bountifully with me."

Use any type of notebook, diary, or blank-paged book you like for your journal. The authors of *The Grief Adjustment Guide* offer the following helpful suggestions for journal keeping.

1. Try to be consistent with your writing. Finding time every day to write at least a short paragraph in your journal is helpful. At the end of a week, review what you have written to see small steps of progress toward grief recovery. Writing at least a line or two every day is the most effective way to keep a journal.
2. Some people write in their journals a few times each week. They review their writing at the end of the week and at the end of each month.
3. If you have trouble getting started, look over the following list of suggested beginnings. Find one that fits what you are feeling or need to express and use it to "jump start" your writing for that day:

Be consistent with your journal entries.

   • My biggest struggle right now is...
   • The thing that really gets me down is...
   • The worst thing about my loss is...
   • When I feel lonely...
   • The thing I most fear is...
   • The most important thing I've learned is...
   • The thing that keeps me from moving on is...
   • I seem to cry most when...
   • I dreamed last night...
   • I heard a song that reminded me of...
   • A new person I've come to appreciate is...
   • I get angry when...
   • Part of the past that keeps haunting me is...

- What I've learned from the past is…
- Guilt feelings seem to occur most when…
- The experiences I miss the most are…
- New experiences I enjoy the most are…
- The changes I least and most like are…
- My feelings sometimes confuse me because…
- I smelled or saw something today that reminded me of…
- A new hope I found today is…
- New strengths I've developed since my loss are…
- I feel close to God today because…
- I am angry at God today because…
- For me to find and have balance, I…
- I got a call or letter from a friend today that…
- My friend, _____, had a loss today, and I…[4]

Start with one word

If one of these starters doesn't fit, then write about what you are feeling. You could start with just one word—misery, longing, hope, or whatever—and then use phrases or sentences to describe that feeling. If you need to, cry as you write, but keep writing until you have nothing more to say about that feeling.

Your journal is yours to say and feel what is in your heart and mind. It is your way of crystallizing the feelings of loss. Dealing with your feelings one at a time, in a written, tangible form is good way to "own" those feelings and to respond to them in an organized way. Grief involves a tangle of feelings, and writing them down is a productive way to isolate and adjust to each one.

Monitor what you write. When you begin to see yourself writing more about what is happening today and less about the one you have lost, you'll know that healing and adjustment indeed are taking place, though they may seem painfully slow in occurring. Look for signs of progress.

✎ **Do you have questions, fears, or concerns about keeping a personal journal? If so, describe them below.**

_____

_____

_____

_____

✎ **Continue working on your memory verse. In the margin describe how remembering this verse can help you when you believe you don't have the strength to tackle some of these choices in loss recovery.**

❦ **As you think about writing in your journal, stop and pray, thanking God that He will give you words—whether many or few—to begin to verbalize your grief and to help you monitor your progress. Thank Him for giving you the strength you need to keep this journal.**

Help Through the Valley

Today's Objective:
You will list strengths you have developed because of your loss and evaluate ways you can use these strengths to help others.

The following chart from *The Grief Adjustment Guide* can assist you in your journey of recovery.[5] The chart shows the curve of emotions and situations that one experiences from the time the loss occurs until the person adjusts to the loss. Review the chart and then answer the questions that pertain to it. Note that the curve resembles a valley; read the Scripture that shows a promise from God about what happens when we go through valleys of loss in our lives.

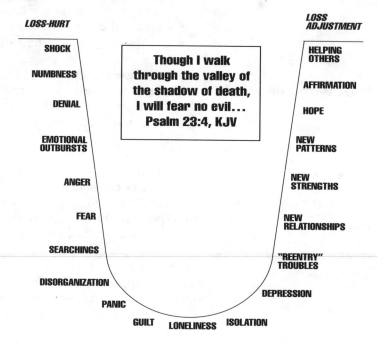

LOSS-HURT

SHOCK
NUMBNESS
DENIAL
EMOTIONAL OUTBURSTS
ANGER
FEAR
SEARCHINGS
DISORGANIZATION
PANIC
GUILT   LONELINESS   ISOLATION

Though I walk through the valley of the shadow of death, I will fear no evil...
Psalm 23:4, KJV

LOSS ADJUSTMENT

HELPING OTHERS
AFFIRMATION
HOPE
NEW PATTERNS
NEW STRENGTHS
NEW RELATIONSHIPS
"REENTRY" TROUBLES
DEPRESSION

After reviewing the chart, take the following actions:

1. Cross out the stages you already have experienced.
2. List ways you have freed yourself from being "stuck" in one phase. (Example: *I have learned to cry freely without letting my tears embarrass me.*)

_____

_____

3. Write some statements about your patterns of dealing with loss. (Examples: *I turn inward instead of outward. I internalize my anger.*)

_____

_____

4. List the strengths you now have because of the loss you have experienced. (Examples: *I'm a survivor! I've learned empathy for others.*)

_____

5. List ways that you can use these new strengths to help others. (Example: *I can consider leading a loss-recovery support group. I am thinking about volunteering in a hospital so I can work with people in loss situations.*)

_____

_____

6. Describe how you feel when you read the promise from the Psalms that appears in the curve of the valley on the chart. (Example: *I can look back and see that God truly has been with me even in the darkest days of my loss.*)

_____

_____

🌱 **Stop and pray, thanking God for the promise that appears in Psalm 23:4 and asking Him to continue to make you aware of His presence.**

DAY 5

Today's Objective:
You will identify the steps to take after completing the six core units of this study.

Ways to further growth

Where Do I Go from Here?

Anita had gone through a grief-recovery support group. She grew through her relationship with the group members, and she completed her workbook material daily. She benefited from learning that other people had undergone experiences similar to her own. She felt a little bewildered about what she should do next. Her support system would no longer be available to her, and she wondered, "What do I do now?"

Anita's feelings are common to those who have done their initial work in loss recovery. In this last day of the six core units of *Recovering from the Losses of Life* LIFE® Support Group Series Edition, we will examine some options for people who are looking for the next steps to take.

Anita's group may continue with the three optional sessions in *Recovering from the Losses of Life* LIFE® Support Group Series Edition. Completing the full nine units in this workbook is the ideal way to make sure that members have all the helps they need to face the issues related to their loss. Anita may want to complete this course in its entirety and then go through the course again to reinforce the concepts that she has learned.

Or, Anita may want to pursue other aspects of her growth. She may find that in completing *Recovering from the Losses of Life* LIFE® Support Group Series she has identified other emotional issues in her life. Or, she may have decided that experiencing healing from her loss has freed her up to disciple others. She may be ready to enhance her understanding of how to know and do God's will in her life, or she may want to learn more about the Bible.

If Anita is not already involved in a regular Bible study at her church, such as a weekly Sunday School class, she would find that regular focus on God's Word important in her life. She may want to participate in her church's discipleship training on a regular basis. She may want to learn to lead support groups in her church so she can help others grow, or she may want to talk with a church staff member about serving her church in some other way. She may find that she needs to spend some time with a qualified Christian counselor to examine some of these grief issues on a one-on-one basis.

In *Treasures from the Dark*, Dwight "Ike" Reighard describes his experience with seeking counseling as he recovered from the loss of his wife and infant. He wrote that he sought a counselor's help because, "we cannot always 'work through' our difficulties alone.... Christian psychological counseling by well-qualified professionals can save our lives.

"Ron (my counselor) led me from a negative approach to a positive one, from a posture of resignation to my circumstances, to one of using those circumstances to rebuild my life and become a more useful, better-prepared servant of God."[6]

Individuals seeking further growth also could benefit from one of the following resources. All are written in the interactive format that *Recovering from the Losses of Life* LIFE® Support Group Series Edition uses. All are intended for group study.

To build self-worth on the forgiveness and love of Jesus Christ:
• *Search for Significance* LIFE® Support Group Series Edition. Helps individuals use the principles from God's Word to replace the false beliefs about themselves that Satan teaches. (Houston: Rapha Publishing), product number 7264-62; Leader's Guide, product number 7269-62.)

To understand how past hurts affect your present actions:
• *Making Peace with Your Past* (Nashville: LifeWay Press), product number 7636-14; Facilitator's Guide (7616-14), and its sequel, *Moving Beyond Your Past* (Nashville: LifeWay Press), product number 7023-03; Facilitator's Guide, product number 7024-03.

To identify and replace codependent behaviors:
• *Untangling Relationships: A Christian Perspective on Codependency*. Helps individuals learn how to make relationships more healthy. (Houston: Rapha Publishing), product number 7202-73; Leader's Guide, 7203-73.

• *Conquering Codependency: A Christ-Centered 12-Step Process* applies the Christ-centered 12 Steps to the patterns called codependency. (Houston: Rapha Publishing) product number 7200-33; Facilitator's Guide, product number 7201-33.

To understand God's will for your life:
• *Experiencing God: Knowing and Doing the Will of God*. Find answers to the often-asked question, "How can I know and do the will of God?" (Nashville: LifeWay Press), product number 7203-00; Leader's Guide, product number 7225-00.

To help you know more about the Bible:
• *Step-by-Step Through the Old Testament*. This self-instructional workbook surveys the Old Testament, provides a framework for understanding and interpreting it, and teaches Bible background. (Nashville: LifeWay Press), product number 7602-71; Leader's Guide, product number 7606-71.

• *Step-by-Step Through the New Testament.* This 13-unit self-instructional workbook surveys the New Testament, provides a framework for understanding and interpreting the New Testament, and teaches Bible background. (Nashville: LifeWay Press, product number 7609-12; Leader's Guide, product number 7610-12.)

To help you learn how to disciple others:
• *MasterLife: Discipleship Training.* This six-month in-depth discipleship process for developing spiritual disciples and leaders trains people to help carry out Christ's vision to make disciples of all nations. For more information write Adult Discipleship and Family Development, MSN 151, 127 Ninth Avenue, North; Nashville, TN 37234.

To help you learn to think the thoughts of Christ:
• *The Mind of Christ.* This course helps the person who is ready for a serious study of what it means to have the thoughts of Christ and to renew his or her mind, as Scripture commands. (Nashville: LifeWay Press), product number 7200-19; Leader's Guide, product number 7200-20.

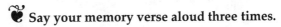 **Say your memory verse aloud three times.**

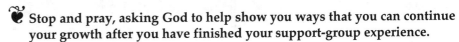 **Stop and pray, asking God to help show you ways that you can continue your growth after you have finished your support-group experience.**

Weekly Work

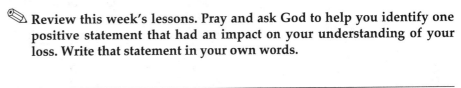 **Review this week's lessons. Pray and ask God to help you identify one positive statement that had an impact on your understanding of your loss. Write that statement in your own words.**

_____

_____

Notes
[1]Ann Kaiser Stearns, *Living Through Personal Crisis* (Chicago: Thomas More Press, 1984), 85, 86..
[2]Therese A. Rando, *Grieving: How to Go On Living When Someone You Love Dies* (Lexington, Massachusetts: Lexington Books, 1988), 281-283, adapted.
[3]Ibid, 284-286, adapted.
[4]Charlotte Greeson, Mary Hollingsworth, and Michael Washburn, *The Grief Adjustment Guide* (Sisters, Oregon: Questar Publishers, Inc., 1990), 90, 91.
[5]Ibid., 68.
[6]Dwight "Ike" Reighard, *Treasures from the Dark* (Nashville: Thomas Nelson, 1990), 88, 93.

Growing Through Loss

Case in point

> ### SEEING THINGS FROM GOD'S PERSPECTIVE
>
> After Ray lost his wife to cancer, he began to work as a hospital volunteer with cancer patients. This helped him move ahead with life because he could help others learn some of the coping skills that worked for him.
>
> After Harry's business failed, he began to take a new look at how he related to employees and to take courses that would help him next time in the workplace.
>
> Ray and Harry did not like what happened to them, but they learned to look at ways God could use their losses to His glory. In this unit you will study helps for people who want to see their circumstances from God's perspective.

What you'll learn

This week you will
• describe survival characteristics that will help you move forward in your grief process.
• identify some ways to evaluate God's role in suffering.
• discover how worshipping God speeds your recovery.
• identify ways you can experience God's timetable in recovery.
• learn to see from God's perspective your recent experience of loss.

What you'll study

Traits of a Survivor	Survival and Faith	Worship and Recovery	Experiencing God's Timetable	Gaining God's Perspective
DAY 1	DAY 2	DAY 3	DAY 4	DAY 5

Memory Verse

This week's verse of Scripture to memorize
"For I know the plans I have for you," declares the Lord, "plans to prosper you and not to harm you, plans to give you hope and a future."
—Jeremiah 29:11

Today's Objective:
You will describe characteristics that will help you survive your loss.

Traits of a Survivor

A fishing crew stays adrift in its small boat for months. Reporters interview the crew members. The resulting story focuses on how they survived.

A plane crashes, and rescuers find it 10 days later. Fourteen people are still living. People ask them the question, "How did you stay alive?"

A car crashes through a guard rail on a deserted mountain road. Five days later rescuers find three injured people surviving. People ask each of them, "How did you make it through that ordeal?"

When we experience a major loss, we can consider the same question because recovery has to do with being a survivor. Some people resolve their crisis and survive. But some don't. What makes the difference? Do some principles exist that could help us face our losses?

✎ **First, let's define a survivor. Before you read further, stop a moment and write your definition of survivor.**

_____

_____

A survivor somehow knows to stay down until the count of nine.

I like how psychiatrist Joy Joffe defines it: "A survivor is a person who, when knocked down, somehow knows to stay down until the count of nine and then to get up differently. The nonsurvivor gets up right away and gets hit again."[1]

Here are some traits of a survivor:
1. Survivors plan ahead, if at all possible, so they can prepare for a transition, loss, or crisis. Survivors have found a way to cope with and master what they experience. Life is full of predictable transitions that can become major losses. Survivors answer the question, "How can I best prepare for this, and what will it mean to me?"

For example, people with children will experience the empty nest. When children leave, the home atmosphere changes, and secondary losses occur. Parents have fewer choices to make, less confusion and noise. Old patterns of shopping, cooking, and scheduling change. Someone else has to meet the needs for communication, affection, and companionship that children once filled. Often the last child leaves home at the same time as mid-life transition or even mid-life crisis occurs. Marital discord may intensify when couples no longer have children around as conversation topics. Yet people can anticipate the empty nest and deal in advance with what it means for them.

Planning in advance

Retirement is a major loss for many people, yet few people anticipate and plan for this event. People sometimes can anticipate physical changes or deterioration. A friend who has ALS—Lou Gehrig's disease—told me that he adjusted his work habits, his type of car, his home's layout, and his family's financial lifestyle so that his wife and he more easily could deal with the next few years. A man with multiple sclerosis changed professions at the early stage of the disease so he could continue working in a job he could manage.

These are people who took charge of potential loss in advance and continued with life. Learning in advance about grief and its traits can help as you go through the process.

✎ **How has this happened for you? In what way have you anticipated changes or losses in your life and responded in advance?**

_____

_____

2. Survivors learn from others' wisdom and experience. They often do this even before they experience a loss but also are eager to learn during the experience itself. They don't try to carry the load themselves but look to others for insights they lack. In the margin box write the initials of people whose wisdom and experience have benefited you.

3. Survivors are not complainers. They deal with their feelings constructively. Even though they may have periodic bouts with feeling sorry for themselves, they don't whine, grumble, complain, or become bitter.

✎ **Are you a complainer? What do you hear yourself saying when difficulties confront you?**

_____

Johnny answered that he often finds himself looking at happy people and saying, "That person wouldn't be so cheerful if he experienced my losses ."

4. Survivors have role models. These role models inspire them through the way they deal with adversity in their own lives. When you see what others can do, that in itself can give you hope. In the margin box write the initials of people who have modeled dealing with adversity.

5. Survivors desire to continue to grow. They stretch mind and attitude to look at something in a new way. Survivors are willing to branch out and learn even if they are comfortable with what they are doing at this time.

✎ **What about you? In what way do you believe you have grown and changed during the past year? Describe below.**

_____

_____

Harry wrote that his business failure caused him to take a new look at how he related to employees and to take courses that would help him next time.

6. Survivors do not blame. Often blame stems from our own feelings of personal responsibility, even though we were not responsible. If a child dies in an accident, the parents may blame each other, the car manufacturer, the doctors, or God. In some cases, other people may in fact be responsible, but to dwell on that issue keeps us stuck in grief. Even though we all feel powerless sometimes, we can decide to take charge of our lives and look for options.

People who have influenced me—

_____

_____

_____

_____

_____

People who have dealt with adversity—

_____

_____

_____

_____

_____

In what way do you tend to blame others for your losses? Describe below.

_____

Stop and pray. Ask God to help you acquire the survival traits that you read about in this day's material.

Begin to memorize this week's Scripture memory verse.

Survival and Faith

In day 1 you identified six traits to help a person survive a loss. Today you will describe three more, including an all-important one—survival and faith.

7. Survivors find a way to live in spite of what has happened to them. They find a way to excel in some area or to express themselves. One Sunday a concert pianist who had been born blind and partially deaf played the offertory in our church. Major league baseball pitcher Jim Abbott has only one good arm and hand. Determination is a necessary trait to survive.

Have you discovered new ways to move ahead in your life when adversity hits? If so describe below.

_____

_____

Ray wrote that, after losing his wife to cancer, he discovered that volunteering to work with cancer patients helped him move ahead with life because he could help others learn some of the coping skills that worked for him.

8. Even in the midst of grief, survivors still can enjoy life and can laugh at times. Yes, a person can laugh even when he or she hurts. Sometimes we laugh at something a deceased person said or did when alive. Often after a funeral, people laugh as they visit with each other.

Have you found that you can laugh about things in the midst of your loss? If so describe below.

_____

_____

9. Survivors have faith in God. Having faith in Jesus Christ and developing a biblical perspective on life is the foundation for survival and recovery. I don't mean that we always understand what happens or that we like it, but we do learn to accept it. Do you understand a cancer ward filled with children under the age of 10? What about the business executive who was honest and who in his company followed biblical teachings, yet his business failed?

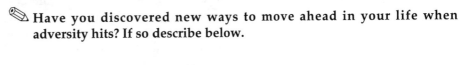

DAY 2

Today's Objective:
You will identify some ways to evaluate God's role in suffering.

We may not always understand what happens, but we learn to accept it.

False assumptions

Some Christians live by assumptions that are not biblically based. Examples:
- Life is fair.
- I can control what happens to me.
- If I follow Christ and His teachings, no tragedy will happen to me.
- If I am suffering, I do so because I am sinning.
- My body was meant to live forever—at least until age 90!
- If I tithe, God will bless me financially.

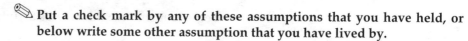 **Put a check mark by any of these assumptions that you have held, or below write some other assumption that you have lived by.**

_____

We need to deal with the questions and issues of life before the deep hurts of life confront us. When we don't, God often gets the blame. Some people need to find a guilty party for their loss, and if they can't find one, they invent one. Sometimes we look at our tragedies and say God has willed them. The Cowlitz Indians believed Mount St. Helens erupted because God was angry about the desecration of their burial grounds. After the massive earthquake in Mexico City in 1985, some people said, "God must be angry."

In her book *Helping People Through Grief*, Delores Kuenning writes that we cannot "suddenly draw from deep reservoirs of faith within ourselves if nothing has been done to nurture our spiritual lives in the past . . .. As human beings made of flesh and blood and bone rather than rubber, steel, or plastic, our reasoning tells us that generally deaths are caused by: errors in human judgment or planning; diseases (some of which are self-imposed); genetic disorders; the evil action of others; violence against self; acts of nature such as earthquake, wind, fire, and flood; and unbending natural laws such as the force of gravity.

Kuenning continues to say that when we "violate the God-given commandments—which are really positive statements designed to help us live a healthy, uncomplicated life—we create the conditions that can wreak havoc with our personal lives. When we disobey God's laws of health, for example, we can expect sickness and the suffering that goes with it. Our bodies are designed by God and require healthful living habits to function properly."[2]

We believe that because we have done something for God, He will insulate us from misfortune.

The other side of blaming God is believing that we are special because of our relationship with Him or because we have done something for Him, and therefore He will insulate us from the misfortunes of life. While He might intervene in our circumstances, we have no right to demand that He do so.

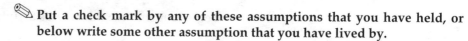 **Have you believed that God would shield you from misfortunes because of something you have done for Him? If so describe below.**

_____

_____

One woman said she believed that because she taught Sunday School for 30 years, she would not lose her eyesight, as she eventually did. One man answered that he believed his family would be free from harm because he was serving God as a missionary. This belief made his anguish all the more painful when his family had to leave the mission field because of his wife's illness.

Pain—death—tragedy—suffering. When they hit us, we feel tormented, and the age-old questions emerge: Why does God allow suffering? Where is He in our suffering? Is He paying attention at all?

✎ **What about you? Have you ever asked any of these questions? Below describe the questions you have raised about God or to God during your loss experience.**

_____

In his book *Where Is God in My Suffering?* Daniel Simundson writes that "when we cry out to God in our times of suffering, we know that we will be heard by one who truly knows what we have gone through. It is a great comfort for a sufferer to know the presence of an understanding and compassionate God, who not only invites our very human prayers but also knows what it is like to be in so much pain. God hears. God understands. God suffers with us. The lament is heard by One who has been there."[3]

We also know that God is omnipotent. That means He is all-powerful. But what does all-powerful mean to you?

✎ **In the margin box write what you think all-powerful means.**

Sometimes we attribute incorrect meanings to God's omnipotence. Does all-powerful mean that He causes every single thing that happens in the world? He is all powerful, but that doesn't necessarily mean everything happens the way He wants it. He created people to have a choice. Because of our choices, things result that are not what God desires. God could not give us the freedom to love Him if we didn't have the freedom to reject Him and His teachings. He wants us to love Him based on our own choice.

Dr. Dwight Carlson wrote that God's self-imposed limitations is a difficult concept to grasp. He says, "But I am convinced that when God created the world, He set laws in motion which even He chooses to honor. The problem for us is that these laws intersect our lives in the most sensitive areas—in our suffering and misfortune."[4]

✎ **Based on what you've read in Day 2 about God's role in suffering, put a check mark beside the statement you believe is true.**

❑ God shields us from misfortune if we've spent a lifetime serving Him.
❑ Hurtful things happen to us because God gave us the freedom of choice.
❑ Everything that happens in the world is just the way God wants it to be.
❑ To recover, we must fully understand everything that happens to us.

Misfortune and suffering happen in life; not even the most active and vibrant Christian is insulated. God doesn't like some of the things that happen to people just as we don't. We may never fully understand why some of life's circumstances occur. What we can understand is that God loves us enough to give us the freedom to choose to love Him. Because we are free to choose this and other things, events result that don't please us or Him. Only the second statement is true.

What *all-powerful* means to me—

_____

_____

_____

_____

_____

We may never fully understand some of life's circumstances.

🍂 Stop and pray. Ask God to help you deal with this sometimes-puzzling concept of His role in suffering. Ask Him to make you aware of how much He cares for you and that He understands how much you hurt.

✎ Continue to memorize this week's Scripture memory verse.

Today's Objective:
You will discover that worshipping God assists your recovery.

Then the Lord answered Job out of the storm.

–Job 38:1

One better, one bitter

Worship and Recovery

What role does worship play in how we deal with the difficulties of life and in our recovery? You might ask: *Why should I want to worship when I feel like dying inside? How can people sing praises and be joyful when their world has collapsed?*

✎ **Have you ever asked how anyone could possibly be expected to worship in the midst of such pain?** ❑ **Yes** ❑ **No**

Read what Richard Exley wrote on this subject:

"We don't worship God because of our losses, but in spite of them. We don't praise Him for the tragedies, but in them. Like Job, we hear God speak to us out of the storm (see Job 38:1 at left.) Like the disciples at sea in a small boat, caught in a severe storm, we too see Jesus coming to us in the fourth watch of the night. We hear Him say, "Take courage! It is I. Don't be afraid" (Matthew 14:27).

"If you've lived for any length of time, you've probably had opportunity to see the different ways people respond to adversity. The same tragedy can make one person better and another person bitter. What makes the difference? Resources. Inner resources developed across a lifetime through spiritual disciplines. *If you haven't worshiped regularly in the sunshine of your life, you probably won't be able to worship in the darkness.* If you haven't been intimate with God in life's ordinariness, it's not likely that you will know how or where to find Him should life hand you some real hardships. *But by the same token, if you have worshiped often and regularly, then you will undoubtedly worship well in the hour of your greatest need.*[5]

✎ **How have you done on this score? Has your worship before your loss been regular or sporadic? Below describe your previous worship patterns.**

_____

_____

How has worship been a part of your loss recovery? What has made worshiping at this time more difficult?

_____

_____

The experience of worship provides the resources we need to draw on when everything around us falls apart. In worship, the focus is not on the person but on God. Do you realize that your understanding of God and how you have worshiped will directly determine how you respond to life's losses?

We are people who usually put faith in formulas. We feel comfortable with predictability, regularity, and assurance. We want God to be this way also, and so we try to create Him in the image of what we want Him to be and what we want Him to do. However, we cannot predict what God will do. Paul reminds us of that in Romans 11:33, appearing at left. God is not uncaring or busy elsewhere. He is neither insensitive nor punitive. He is supreme, sovereign, loving, and sensitive.

> O the depth of the riches both of the wisdom and knowledge of God! how unsearchable are his judgments, and his ways past finding out!
> –Romans 11:33, KJV

I too have unanswered questions about some of the events in my life. But all of life's trials, problems, crises, and suffering occur by divine permission. God allows suffering for His purpose and for His reasons. He controls the universe, and He permits suffering. God is free to do as He desires, and He doesn't have to give us explanations or share His reasons. He doesn't owe us. He already has given His Son and His Holy Spirit to strengthen and guide us.

What God allows us to experience is for our growth. God has arranged the seasons of nature to produce growth, and He arranges the experiences of the seasons of our lives for growth also. He does not always give us what we think we need or want but what will produce growth.

A woman I counseled was upset because a friend had suggested she thank God for the problems she was experiencing. "How can I thank God for this loss?" she asked me. "It's disrupted my whole life!"

I asked her whether she thought her friend meant "to thank God for this specific loss as though it were good in and of itself, or to thank God for using this so that you have an opportunity to change and grow."

The woman pondered this question for a moment. I continued, "I know it hurts, and you and your family wish it had never occurred, but it did. So the past can't be changed and you feel out of control. Perhaps you can't change what happens in the future, but you can control your response to whatever occurs."

She thought about it, and in time she thanked God for being with her and allowing her this time of growth. She said, "I thought about the choices I had, I could depend on God, thank Him, praise Him, and allow Him to work through me. Or I could remain bitter and angry. Praising God didn't seem so bad when I considered the alternative."

Can you praise Him?

✎ **What can you thank God for in your loss? Below write your answer.**

_____

_____

_____

❧ **Stop and pray, thanking God for the matters you wrote about in the exercise above. Ask Him to show you how He can work through you.**

✎ Continue work on this week's memory verse, Jeremiah 29:11. Look back at page 86 if you need to refresh your memory. In the margin write how the promise of the verse can help you learn to worship God.

<table>
</table>

DAY 4

Today's Objective:
You will identify some ways to experience God's timetable in your recovery.

Experiencing God's Timetable

What kind of growth can we expect as we go through this journey of recovery? Lloyd Ogilvie suggests some of the things we can learn as we go through the difficult times in life that he calls valleys.

✎ In the next three paragraphs, underline phrases that could represent a goal for you in loss recovery.

- "First, it has been in the valleys of waiting for answers to my prayers that I have made the greatest strides in growing in the Lord's grace.
- "Second, it's usually in retrospect, after the strenuous period is over, that I can look back with gratitude for what I've received of the Lord Himself. I wouldn't trade the deeper trust and confidence I experienced from the valley for a smooth and trouble-free life.
- "Third, I long to be able to remember what the tough times provide in my relationship with the Lord, so that when new valleys occur, my first reaction will be to thank and praise the Lord in advance for what is going to happen in and through me as a result of what happens to me. I really want my first thought to be, 'Lord, I know You didn't send this, but You have allowed it and will use it as a part of working all things together for good. I trust You completely, Lord!'"[6]

✎ Below describe anything that you believe keeps you from meeting any of the goals you underlined.

_____

_____

You might have underlined such phrases as "can look back with gratitude" or "my first reaction will be to thank and praise the Lord in advance." You might have written something like this: "My first reaction now is to berate the Lord in advance instead of thanking Him. I need to overcome my bitterness."

Gratitude doesn't mean that we don't suffer the pain of a loss.

An attitude of gratitude doesn't mean that we don't suffer the pain of a loss. When we have suffered a loss, we feel like the disciples did when they were adrift in that small boat during the storm on the Sea of Galilee. The waves throw us about. Just as we get our legs under us, something hits us from another direction. The disciples struggled on the Sea of Galilee, and we struggle on the sea of life. All of us are afraid of capsizing. All we see are waves that seem to grow larger each moment. We're afraid. However, Jesus spoke to the disciples and He speaks to us today with the same message, "It is I; don't be afraid" (John 6:20).

We ask God, "Where are You?" but He always is there in the midst of the crisis. We ask Him, "When? When will You answer?" Our cry is the same as the

How long , O Lord? Will you forget me forever? How long will you hide your face from me? How long must I wrestle with my thoughts and every day have sorrow in my heart? How long will my enemy triumph over me?

–Psalm 13:1-2

Since ancient times no one has heard, no ear has perceived, no eye has seen any God besides you, who acts on behalf of those who wait for him. You come to the help of those who gladly do right, who remember your ways.

–Isaiah 64:4-5

Wait on the Lord: be of good courage, And he shall strengthen thine heart: wait, I say, on the Lord.

–Psalm 27:14, KJV

But they that wait upon the Lord shall renew their strength; they shall mount up with wings as eagles, they shall run, and not be weary, and they shall walk, and not faint.

–Isaiah 40:31, KJV

But I trust in you, O Lord; I say, "You are my God." My times are in your hands."

–Psalm 31:14-15

psalmist's cry, which appears in the margin. We want Him to act according to our timetable, but the Scripture says, "Be still before the Lord and wait patiently for him" (Psalm 37:7). We become restless in waiting, and to block out the pain of waiting, we often are driven to frantic activity. This does not help, but resting before the Lord does.

We often do not believe that God is doing anything to help us recover because we want recovery now. The instant-solution philosophy of our society often keeps us from having a proper perspective of God. We complain about waiting a few days or weeks, but to God a day is as a thousand years and a thousand years as an instant. God works in hidden ways, even when you and I are totally frustrated by His apparent lack of response. We merely are unaware that He is active. In the margin read the words of Isaiah for people then and now.

God has a reason for everything He does and a timetable for when He does it. Reflect on your memory verse, "'For I know the plans I have for you,' declares the Lord, 'plans to prosper you and not to harm you, plans to give you hope and a future'"(Jeremiah 29:11).

✎ **Below describe how Jeremiah 29:11 can help you be more comfortable with God's timetable.**

_____

_____

You may have answered something like this: *When I realize that God has plans that are hopeful for me, I can try to have patience to realize that He alone knows when He will enact those plans.*

Dwight "Ike" Reighard wrote this about following God's timetable in overcoming the deaths of his wife Cindy and their infant: "Wounds heal slowly, and at times we must just be with the pain and wait for a pain-free day. What I can tell you is that the pain-free day will come. Though you may experience setbacks, little by little the open wound will close…. Overcoming loss is a process; deep wounds are not healed overnight. Grief recovery requires patiently waiting for things to get better; remember that God is in the waiting." Reighard cited the two verses appearing left that he said helped him with this waiting.[7]

Give yourself permission not to know what, not to know how, and not to know when. Even though you feel adrift on the turbulent ocean, God is holding you and knows the direction of your drift.

Giving yourself permission to wait can give you hope. God has the right to ask us to wait for weeks and months and even years if necessary. During that time, when we do not receive the answer and/or solution we think we need, He gives us His presence. In the bottom verse appearing in the margin, read about that promise of His presence.

❦ **Stop and pray, asking God to help you rest in His promise that your wounds one day will heal. Ask Him to help you operate on His timetable instead of on your own. You may wish to use the words of Psalm 31:14-15 as you express to God your faith in the midst of pain.**

✎ Evaluate your growth in this area. Can you think of times during your recovery that you have given yourself permission to wait? If so, describe below, and then give yourself a pat on the back for making this brave step of waiting on God's timetable.

_____

_____

_____

✎ Review your Scripture memory verse for this week and your Scripture memory verses for the previous units.

Gaining God's Perspective

Today's Objective:
You will learn to see from God's perspective your recent experience of loss.

The following verse perhaps best summarizes the ability to develop a biblical perspective on our lives: "Consider it all joy, my brethren, when you encounter various trials, knowing that the testing of your faith produces endurance" (James 1:2-3, NASB).

Reading a passage like this is easy. Putting these verses into practice, however, is another thing indeed. Can we really consider it all joy when we encounter trials because we know that the testing of our faith produces endurance? Just how easy is that to do?

✎ On a scale of 0 to 10, with 0 being "not at all" and 10 being "I do this routinely," how close are you now to putting James 1:2-3 into practice? On the scale below, indicate your progress.

_____

0   5   10

Make up your mind

In the James 1:2-3 passage, what does the word *consider* actually mean? It refers to an internal attitude. It means "make up your mind." Another way you might translate James 1:2-3 is, "Make up your mind to look on adversity as something to welcome or be glad about because you know that God will help you to grow even through suffering." You have the power to decide what your attitude will be.

You can say, "That's terrible. That is the last thing I wanted to happen in my life. Why did it have to happen now? Why me?"

The other way of considering the same difficulty is to say, "It's not what I wanted or expected, but it's here. I may have some difficult times, but how can I make the best of them?"

Never deny the pain or hurt you might have to go through, but always ask, "What can I learn from it? How can I grow through this? How can I use it for God's glory?"

*"I can find a better way
of responding to this."*

The verb tense used in the word *consider* means to act decisively. It does not mean: "Well, I'll just give up. I'm stuck with this problem. That's the way life is." The verb tense indicates you will have to go against your natural inclination to see the trial as a negative force. When you begin to think negative, bitter thoughts, you will have to remind yourself, *No, I think I can find a better way of responding to this. Lord, I really want You to help me see it from a different perspective.* Then your mind will shift to a more constructive response. Changing your thought patterns often takes a lot of work on your part.

God created us with both the capacity and the freedom to determine how we will respond to unexpected incidents life brings our way. You honestly may wish a certain event never had occurred, but you cannot change facts.

During times of crisis as well as during all the other times of life, our stability comes from our Lord. We see these promises in God's Word. Read the three verses appearing in the margin to learn about that source of stability in our lives.

Now to Him who is able to establish you according to my gospel and the preaching of Jesus Christ, according to the revelation of the mystery which has been kept secret for long ages past.
–Romans 16:25, NASB

Then he said to them, "Go, eat of the fat, drink of the sweet, and send portions to him who has nothing prepared; for this day is holy to our Lord. Do not be grieved, for the joy of the Lord is your strength."
–Nehemiah 8:10, NASB

And He shall be the stability of your times, A wealth of salvation, wisdom, and knowledge; The fear of the Lord is his treasure.
–Isaiah 33:6, NASB

✎ **In each of the three verses underline the phrase that indicates that God is the source of our stability.**

✎ **Think about the following three questions that you read on the previous page, and answer them as they apply to you.**

What can you learn from your most recent loss, or what would you like to learn?

_____

_____

_____

How can you grow because of this loss experience, or how would you like to grow?

_____

_____

_____

How can you use for God's glory what you experienced?

_____

_____

_____

_____

Yes, recovery is possible. God wants us to recover, and He has provided a way for us to recover!

✎ **Below write this week's Scripture verse from memory.**

_____

_____

_____

❦ Stop and pray, thanking God that He can show you ways to use your loss for His glory.

Weekly Work

✎ Review this week's lessons. Pray and ask God to help you identify one positive statement that had an impact on your understanding of your loss. Write that statement in your own words.

_____

_____

_____

Notes

[1] As quoted in Ann Kaiser Stearns, _Coming Back_ (New York: Ballantine Books, 1988), 157.

[2] Delores Kuenning, _Helping People Through Grief_ (Minneapolis: Bethany House Publishers, 1987), 20, 21.

[3] Daniel Simundson, _Where Is God in My Suffering?_ (Minneapolis: Augsburg Publishing House, 1983), 28, 29.

[4] Dwight Carlson, _When Life Isn't Fair_ (Eugene, Oregon: Harvest House Publishers, 1989), 38.

[5] John Killinger, _For God's Sake—Be Human_ (Dallas: Texas: Word Incorporated, 1970). As quoted in Richard Exley, _The Rhythm of Life_ (Tulsa: Honor Books, 1987), 108.

[6] Lloyd John Ogilvie, _Why Not? Accept Christ's Healing and Wholeness_ (Old Tappan, New Jersey: Fleming H. Revell Company, 1985), 162.

[7] Dwight "Ike" Reighard, _Treasures from the Dark_ (Nashville: Thomas Nelson, 1990), 182-183.

A Special Kind of Pain

Case in point

FEAR OF TRYING AGAIN

When Jim's wife divorced him to marry her employer, Jim was devastated, but gradually he began to date again. However, he was unsuccessful in his new relationships.

One day Jim explained: "I guess I'm still angry at my wife for leaving me. But I can't make her pay for what she did to me, and I can't take my anger out on her. So that's probably why these new relationships aren't working out. I like the women I date, but I don't treat them well. I get angry at them, and I'm often rude. That's just not me. I guess I'm trying to get back at my wife by taking my anger out on these other women, and that isn't good for them or for me. I guess I try to hurt them first because I'm afraid they may hurt me the way my wife did. And I don't ever want to be hurt like that again!"

Fortunately Jim had the insight to understand how he was reacting to the pain of his loss and to try to control his reaction. This unit will help you understand how you can react to your special type of a pain in a more Christ-honoring way.

What you'll learn

This week you will
- describe how a broken relationship can cause you to fear beginning new relationships;
- identify some stages that are predictable in your recovery;
- identify some common mistakes people make after a relationship ends;
- describe how making a list of your hurts and resentments can help you say goodbye;
- identify how making a list of all your hurts and resentments can help you forgive.

What you'll study

When Pain Clouds the Issue	Some Predictable Stages	Some Common Mistakes	Facing Reality	The Forgiveness Process
DAY 1	DAY 2	DAY 3	DAY 4	DAY 5

Memory Verse

This week's verses of Scripture to memorize
Since, then, you have been raised with Christ, set your hearts on things above, where Christ is seated at the right hand of God. Set your minds on things above, not on earthly things.

—Colossians 3:1-2

Today's Objective:
You will describe how a broken relationship can cause you to fear beginning new relationships.

When Pain Clouds the Issue

Often a special kind of pain clouds the issue of recovery from loss. We feel heartache, disappointment, loneliness, or numbness because a friendship, engagement, or marriage has ended. Sometimes another type of estrangement is involved in the loss: the person who died may have been abusive or neglectful. Perhaps some rift had prevented us from talking to the individual for months or years, and now he or she is dead. We feel puzzled, angry, and even guilty for the strain in the relationship, since the person died with things unresolved.

Some people face these types of losses squarely, learn from them, override their fears, and move on. Those who were involved in some type of break-up grow to trust and love again. But others allow their emotional wounds to remain perpetually open; they give in to their fears by withdrawing from intimate relationships. The trauma of love lost is one of life's most painful hurts, and the apprehension about loving again is one of life's greatest fears.

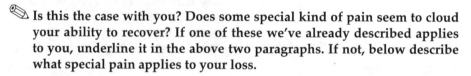 **Is this the case with you? Does some special kind of pain seem to cloud your ability to recover? If one of these we've already described applies to you, underline it in the above two paragraphs. If not, below describe what special pain applies to your loss.**

_____

_____

When you trust another person with your feelings of love and affection, and the relationship ends—either by breakup or by death—your life seems to stand still for a while. Some of the men and women who hurt the most are those who still are attached deeply to former spouses or fiancés and want the relationship to be restored. They feel desperate, totally out of control, and willing to do almost anything to keep their partners. But they have no control over their loved ones' decisions.

Afraid to try again

Once your intimate relationship ends, a part of you wants to try again with a new relationship. But another part of you says, "Don't. It isn't worth the risk!" You fear the past will recur and your new relationship also may end in a painful breakup. Or you are afraid you always will feel the loss and pain of your previous relationship and never will be able to reach out and love again. You fear even more intensely whenever you relive what occurred. Every time the painful scenario replays in your memory, the emotional sledgehammer crashes down on you again.

Below describe what fears you are experiencing about relationships at the present time.

_____

_____

The fear of reliving the past interferes with the normal process of building a new relationship. This fear creates a hesitancy to invest energy, love, and

Feeling trapped

transparency in a new relationship. Many people who are afraid to move ahead in a new relationship also are afraid to remain behind without anyone to love. They feel trapped between the fear of loving again and the fear of never being loved again.

✎ **Think back on the first loss you experienced in a relationship. How did this affect future relationships? Describe below.**

_____

_____

One said: "I once felt so devastated by the loss of a friendship that I acted hurtfully and rude to a potential new friend who invited me to lunch with her. I hadn't meant to be unkind, but the fear of experiencing another rejection overpowered me."

Like a death

The loss created by a broken friendship can be devastating. Twice in my adult life I have experienced such pain. I hurt, wondering what went wrong. If you have numerous close friends, this type of loss may not bother you greatly, since you have other relationships to which you can turn. But for the person who has only one or two close friends, the severance of a relationship can feel like a death.

Other emotions can feed the fear of loving again. One of these emotions is guilt—the feeling that you have failed yourself, your Lord, or the other person. Unresolved guilt damages self-esteem, and low self-esteem produces greater fear. If you feel guilty about a broken relationship, you can identify whether the feelings are based on reality (such as breaking a commitment or acting irresponsibility toward the other person) or imagination (taking the blame for something that was not really your responsibility).

Why do these broken relationships hit us so hard? Part of the happiness that emerges from a close, loving relationship involves being loved by the other person. Consider the parent-child relationship. Usually, it is a two-way love relationship. If your father dies, you know he didn't die because he stopped caring for you. He simply died; you accept that.

"What was wrong with me?"

But when a relationship breaks up, things are different. The love and care that once existed for you has dried up. It has vanished into thin air. The person still exists. You still may see each other occasionally at work or at church or in your daily routine. That makes the loss even more difficult. And what if he or she begins to date your best friend? You wonder, *Why is she good enough for him but I wasn't?* Many of these same emotions occur with the death of someone with whom you've been estranged. Feelings of "What was wrong with me?" and "Why couldn't I have been worthy in his/her sight?" crop up.

When breakups occur, you long for the relationship you once had (or could have had). For some, this longing becomes an obsession dominating every waking moment. The feeling of being out of control is particularly devastating, since you usually can do little to restore the situation. You can beg, plead, offer bribes, and so on, but to no avail. Nothing seems to work, nothing will work, and nothing does work. You feel abandoned, forsaken betrayed, and all alone.

✎ **Below describe some of the things that you may have tried unsuccessfully to restore a broken or estranged relationship.**

_____

_____

Jesus knew rejection

Thinking about Jesus' experiences with rejection can help us proceed in our recovery. Jesus Christ—the only sinless person who ever lived—did not escape the type of abandonment that you feel. His closest friends did not understand Him and would not stay awake and pray with Him during His anguish. One of them betrayed Him and turned Him over to be arrested and killed. His mother and siblings had their doubts about Him. While dying on the cross, He felt that even His Father had forsaken Him.

✎ **Below describe how you feel when you realize that Jesus knows your sorrows regarding the pain of loss and abandonment.**

_____

_____

❦ **Stop and pray. Ask God to help you remember that you are not alone during the times that you feel devastated about the pain of a lost or estranged relationship.**

✎ **Begin to memorize Colossians 3:1-2, this unit's Scripture memory verses.**

DAY 2

Today's Objective:
You will identify some stages that are predictable in your recovery.

Some Predictable Stages

Like the grief you experience when a person dies, the stages you will go through to recover from a lost or estranged relationship are somewhat predictable. These stages constitute the normal process of recovery.

Keep in mind that the stages we identify here do not occur in an automatic or consistent order. They vary in their length and intensity, depending on the duration and strength of the relationship. When the breakup is not your doing or desire, the result is even more intense.

You usually go through six stages when a relationship falls apart. Your pain will be the greatest during the first three stages. As you move through each stage, the intensity of your pain will diminish. The further along the path you proceed, the less fear you will experience. The worst thing to have happen to you is to get stuck in a stage and not complete the process. Some of these stages overlap, and you may move back and forth between them for a while. This is quite normal. It is part of the healing process.

Stage One: Shock. When you first lose a relationship, you feel overwhelmed by shock. Even when you have anticipated a breakup or a divorce, the reality of the loss has a unique effect. Some people are unable to carry on their day-to-day activities; even eating and sleeping are chores.

You may experience an intense fear of being alone or of being abandoned forever, but you need to experience these feelings to move through the healing process. At this stage, you need to have other people around you, whether or not you feel like having them around. Just the presence of other people can help ease the fear of loneliness.

✎ **In the margin box write the initials of people with whom you have surrounded yourself during this stage. If you have tried to go through this stage alone, write the initials of people you will seek out to help you through the shock.**

Stage Two: Grief. The grief stage may be extensive. It includes mourning the loss of what you shared together and what you could have shared together.

✎ **In the next three paragraphs underline the harmful thoughts you have had about yourself in the aftermath of your loss.**

During this time, you may feel and express the anger we described earlier. You may be angry at yourself, at God, and at others who don't understand your grief. You may become depressed about the broken relationship and about the hopelessness of relationships in the future. You may believe that nobody understands. Please be aware that individuals who have gone through this type of devastation understand every aspect of it. They understand the feelings of abandonment, self-blame, other-blame, anger, guilt, the knifelike anguish, and pain.

Many people experience mild paranoia. They make statements like "Everyone is talking about me," "I can tell they're avoiding me," and "No one wants to be around me." The person often believes these statements, and worse yet, in some narrow, unloving churches, these statements sometimes are true. People commonly feel self-conscious during this time.

After a rejection you may think: "Everybody hates me" and "God hates me." These thoughts just are not true. You are God's creation for whom He sent His Son to die. Nothing can happen to you that can cause Him to hate you; nothing in your past is so terrible that God cannot use you. When others respond to you in a hurtful manner, they don't do this because of some defect in you. They may be self-conscious and don't know what to say. Few people actually know how to respond to someone involved in a broken relationship.

✎ **In the margin box describe any additional harmful thoughts you have experienced.**

You can practice thought-stopping so that reality has a chance to gain a foothold in your life once again. Notice the following examples of negative thoughts and how you can counter them to bring your life back into balance. You may benefit from monitoring and charting your own thoughts.

Negative Thought	Answers
I need him.	I want him back, but I don't need him. I need food, water, and shelter to survive. I don't need a man to survive. Thinking in terms of "needs" makes me vulnerable.

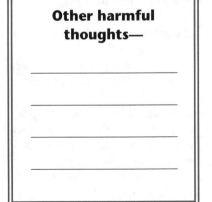

People who can surround me—

_____

_____

_____

_____

People think others are talking about them and avoiding them.

Other harmful thoughts—

_____

_____

_____

_____

Stopping harmful thoughts

Negative Thoughts	Answers
This always happens to me, and it never will change.	Just because it happened in one case doesn't mean it has happened or will happen in every case.
This is terrible, awful, horrible.	These are labels I add to the facts. The labels don't change anything, and they make me feel worse.
I must have someone to love me.	Loving and being loved is nice, but making this a condition to happiness is a way of putting myself down.
I'm too ugly to find someone else.	Thinking like this is self-defeating and stops me from trying. Besides, "too" is a relative concept, not some absolute standard.
I can't stand being alone.	I can stand difficulties—as I have in the past. I just don't like them.
He made me depressed.	No one can make me feel depressed. I make myself depressed by the way I'm thinking.[1]

You will keep in perfect peace him whose mind is steadfast, because he trusts in you.

–Isaiah 26:3

Be renewed in the spirit of your mind, and put on the new self, which in the likeness of God has been created in righteousness and holiness of the truth.

–Ephesians 4:23-24, NASB

Since, then, you have been raised with Christ, set your hearts on things above, where Christ is seated at the right hand of God. Set your minds on things above, not on earthly things.

–Colossians 3:1-2

We demolish arguments and every pretension that sets itself up against the knowledge of God, and we take captive every thought to make it obedient to Christ.

–2 Corinthians 10:5

Finally, brothers, whatever is true, whatever is noble, whatever is right, whatever is pure, whatever is lovely, whatever is admirable—if anything is excellent or praiseworthy—think about such things.

–Philippians 4:8

 **Now it's your turn to try. In the blanks below write one of your frequent negative thoughts. Beside it write a thought stopper you can use to keep it from getting a toehold.**

Negative Thought	Answer
_____	_____
_____	_____

You can have hope in spite of recurring thoughts. You can evict these harmful thoughts from your life. Take three specific steps to change thought patterns.

- **First, pray out loud.** Share your concern, and describe specifically what you want God to do with these thoughts.
- **Second, read aloud the Scriptures appearing in the margin.** (One of these is our memory passage for the week.) These describe how we can control our thought life.
- **Third, identify one of the most persistent thoughts**—the one that pops into your head more frequently than any of the others. Select a time when you are not upset. Without becoming angry, say the statement out loud. If you can't, that's OK. In time, you will be able to do this. As you say the last word of the statement (such as, "How could she have been so unfair?"), slam a book or ruler loudly on a table, or clap your hands. Repeat the sentence and move the noise back one word each time you repeat the bothersome thought. In time, you will interrupt this thought before it has a chance to begin. As this happens, thank God for taking this thought from your life.

✎ Below write the statement that you will use to practice your thought-stopping activity. After you write it practice the three-step process to stop the thought.

_____

_____

❦ Stop and pray. Ask God to help you erase harmful thoughts from your life so that your recovery can proceed.

✎ In the margin write your Scripture memory verses for this unit.

Some Common Mistakes

DAY 3

Today's Objective:
You will identify some common mistakes people make after a relationship ends.

In day 2 you identified the first two stages of recovering from loss of a relationship. In day 3 you will identify the third stage—**Blame.** You may hold feelings of blame, accompanied by anger, toward your former spouse, friend, fiancé, or dating partner—or even toward yourself. You may be surprised at your own behavior as you attempt to rid yourself of these feelings. You may engage in compulsive behaviors such as shopping or eating binges, alcohol abuse, or sexual immorality. You may make poor decisions at this stage out of fear of rejection, or feelings of personal inadequacy.

When Jim's wife divorced him to marry her employer, Jim was devastated, but gradually he began to date again. However, he was unsuccessful in his new relationships. One day Jim explained: "I guess I'm still angry at my wife for leaving me. But I can't make her pay for what she did to me, and I can't take my anger out on her. So that's probably why these new relationships aren't working out. I like the women I date, but I don't treat them well. I get angry at them, and I'm rude. That's just not me. I guess I'm trying to get back at my wife by taking my anger out on other women, and that isn't good for them or for me. I try to hurt them first because I'm afraid they may hurt me the way my wife did, and I don't ever want to be hurt like that again!" Fortunately, Jim had the insight to figure out what he was doing, and eventually he moved out of this stage.

Generalization

During the grief and blame stages, some common mistakes can hinder recovery. Generalizing after any broken relationship is easy to do. You take one isolated belief or experience and make it apply to life in general. Many times I've heard my counselees say, "All women are money-minded," "All men are losers," "All men are sex animals," "All women are full of emotions. They can't think." Such generalizations become immobilizers.

✎ **What generalizations have you used? In the paragraph above underline those that apply to you, or list others below.**

_____

_____

People often fall into the trap of living by a self-fulfilling prophecy. Perhaps you have heard someone say—or you have said—"I'll never find anyone else. I'm stuck in life. I'll always be single now." Or you may have said, "I must not be worthy to be anyone's friend." Faulty beliefs like these blind us from seeing the possibilities around us. They give us an attitude and a look of defeat. These prophecies do nothing but undermine and cripple relationships.

✎ **In the margin box describe any self-fulfilling prophecies you have used.**

Another mistake we tend to make after a broken relationship is having unrealistic expectations. When things don't happen according to our rigid set of beliefs, we perpetuate a life of disappointment. We use expectations such as these for ourselves and for other people:

- "I have to be perfect for anyone to love me."
- "If I don't meet all of his needs, he won't love me."
- "If she cares about me, she will _____ and she won't _____."
- "If he reminds me of my former spouse, he's not worth being with."

✎ **Below describe any unrealistic expectations you have had for yourself or for other people.**

_____

_____

A constant pity party

Wallowing in self-pity frequently follows a severed relationship. But indulging in self-pity blocks recovery and keeps others from getting close. An earlier memory verse in this study reminds us that "As a person thinks within himself, so he is." If we engage in a pity party in our thoughts, we will become the piteous, miserable people we think ourselves to be. Who wants to be friends with or date someone who thinks of himself or herself as a loser? That kind of attitude does nothing to draw people to us.

✎ **Below draw a picture of yourself looking pitiful as you might after you wallow in self-pity about your loss. In the second box draw a picture of yourself as you might look if you set aside this attitude.**

Obsessed with busyness

Sometimes we are unable to face ourselves because of what has happened. Sometimes we refer to such people as _runners_. They continually are on the go doing things to avoid having to deal with their situations and their feelings. They increase familiar patterns—working, playing, staying out each night, sleeping, watching TV, or using alcohol and other drugs. Sometimes these people even immerse themselves in church activities just so they can stay occupied. That way they don't have to take an honest look at themselves and evaluate what went wrong in the relationship. People who are obsessed with busyness harm themselves as much as if they were lethargic or withdrawn.

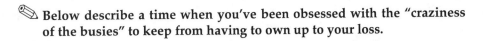 **Below describe a time when you've been obsessed with the "craziness of the busies" to keep from having to own up to your loss.**

_____

_____

Revenge loving

A common mistake designed both to overcome the pain of the loss and to strike back is revenge loving. The hurt person plunges into a new relationship prematurely out of anger. Revenge loving can manifest itself in three different styles.

1. We engage in a new relationship simply to make the other person jealous.
2. We act toward the new person the way the former partner treated us. If I was the abused person, I become the abuser in the new relationship.
3. We develop a relationship in which we are in control so no one ever can hurt us again.

In all three of these revenge styles, both you and the new person end up hurt, unhappy, and dissatisfied.

Magnification

Magnification is another trap that occurs after a broken relationship. In magnification, you begin to think about the person you lost and imagine that he or she is having a great time while you live in despair and discouragement. You feel limited and constrained, while you are sure the other person is living life to its fullest. The major phrase in your vocabulary is, "He is probably..." or "She is probably..." Magnification easily leads to martyrdom if you let it. We all have a choice in how we respond.

Rebounding

Many people move into rebounding after a relationship. One young woman described her process of rebounding this way: "I'm always jumping into one relationship after another—and unfortunately, one bed after another. I don't like myself for doing this, and it makes me feel even worse about the relationship I lost. I've decided to find some more constructive things to do with my time. It hurts, but I'm sure I can grow through this experience. I don't want to be chained to him forever, and I think I have been."

Idealization

Both rejecters and rejectees use idealization. Rejecters use the technique to rationalize why they broke off the relationship with the other person. Rejectees use it as a means to deaden the pain of the loss. They say: "He really had a lot of problems and defects, or she wasn't who or what she said. In the long run, I think it's better that I look around and find someone else." But the standards they set for this new person are totally unrealistic. Possibly they set excessive standards to protect themselves from ever having another relationship because they would never find the perfect person they imagine.

On the other hand, many people choose someone just like their former partner, spouse, or friend. These replacements probably disappoint just as the previous partners did. But something drives these hurt individuals to prove that they can have relationships with people like this. This is why daughters with nonaffirming, aloof, distant fathers choose husbands with exactly these same traits.

In the margin by the four traits you just read about—revenge loving, magnification, rebounding, and idealization—put a check mark if you've ever found yourself in any of these traps. Then below your check mark, describe how that mistake impacted you.

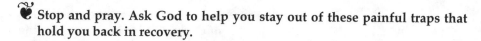 Stop and pray. Ask God to help you stay out of these painful traps that hold you back in recovery.

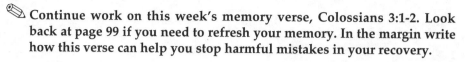 Continue work on this week's memory verse, Colossians 3:1-2. Look back at page 99 if you need to refresh your memory. In the margin write how this verse can help you stop harmful mistakes in your recovery.

Facing Reality

DAY 4

Today's Objective:
You will describe how making a list of your hurts and resentments can help you say goodbye.

Stage Four: Goodbye. Goodbyes are often difficult to face. This is when you really finally admit to yourself, "The relationship is over; this person is out of my life, and I have to go on." Numerous people get stuck on the threshold of this stage. Some of them seem to move ahead, yet three weeks later they are asking the same questions and making the same statements about a reconciliation that never will happen. They are unwilling to say the final goodbye.

How do you say goodbye? Some of the same suggestions you read in unit 5 about saying goodbye can apply when you suffer a special kind of pain—ending a relationship with a friend, date, fiancé, or spouse. These also can apply when you are coping with the death of someone to whom you have been estranged. Look back at unit 5. Then read in days 4 and 5 these same suggestions as they apply to these kinds of relationships.

Perhaps the initial step in overcoming anger and resentment is to identify the hurt, anger, and resentment. One divorced man wrote:
- I am so angry at you for your lies and infidelities.
- I resent the fact that I have to pay you spousal support. You should be the one to have to pay this because of what you did.
- I am wounded by your betrayal of me and our wedding vows.
- I am angry that you have the kids and that they are being influenced by your lousy lifestyle and lack of morals.

Someone who's been dumped by a long-time date could write:
- I resent the fact that you took so much of my time. I could have been dating others, but I restricted myself to you and look where it got me!
- I feel angry because you told me that I was the one for you.
- I feel hurt because of the embarrassment our break-up is causing me.

Someone recovering from the death of an abusive parent might state:
- I resent the fact that you died before I had a chance to talk to you about how much you hurt me when I was a child.
- I feel angry because you died before I graduated from college. I wanted you to see what I made of my life.
- I resent how much my relationship with you impacts me as an adult: my marriage and my relationship with my own children.

Often, when a person begins listing these resentments, buried hurts and feelings begin climbing through the barriers. This list is for your own use; avoid sharing it with anyone else except God. This is not an easy experience. You may find it very emotionally draining, but it is necessary.

On separate paper, make your own list like the previous paragraphs suggest. Write down all of the buried hurts and resentments which God brings to your mind.

After you have made your list, go into a room and set up two chairs facing each other. Sit in one chair and imagine the other person is sitting opposite you listening to what you are thinking. Read your list out loud. Let your tone and voice inflections register the feelings you have. Don't be concerned about editing what you are saying. Just get it out.

Some people keep their list for days and add to it as things occur to them. Others find that they benefit from sitting down and reading this several times. When you have concluded reading your list, spend a few minutes in prayer sharing these feelings with God and thanking Him for understanding what you are experiencing and for His presence in your life to help you overcome the feelings.

Stop and pray, asking God to help you to express your buried hurts and resentments in the way the previous paragraph just described.

DAY 5

Today's Objective:
You will describe how making a list of all your hurts and resentments can help you to forgive.

Keep writing until you have drained all pockets of resentment.

The Forgiveness Process

To become a free person and to move forward in life, you can take one more step to relinquish your anger and resentment. That step is **forgiveness.**

We usually have our own set of reasons for not forgiving. We say we cannot forgive. By identifying the reasons why we object to forgiving the people who have hurt us, we can allow forgiveness into our lives. We will describe a practical method to forgive. After we explain, we'll provide an activity to help you take that step.

To become willing to forgive, you take a blank sheet of paper and write at the top, using the name of your former partner, "Dear _____." Under this, write the words, "I forgive you for ____." Then complete the sentence by stating something the person did that still hurts and angers you. Then capture the first thought that comes to mind after you write the sentence. It may be a feeling or thought that actually contradicts the forgiveness you try to express. It may be an emotional rebuttal or protest to what you just wrote. Keep writing the "I forgive you for _____" statements for every thought or feeling that arises to the surface.

Your list may fill one page or more. Don't be discouraged if your angry protests contradict the concept of forgiveness or are so firm that you believe you have not expressed any forgiveness at all. You are in the process of forgiving this person, so keep writing until you have drained all your buried pockets of resentment. Once again, show this list to no one, but using an empty chair, read the list aloud as though the person were sitting there and listening to you.

The next page contains a sample of what a woman wrote to her former husband, who had divorced her.

Dear Jim:

I forgive you for not being willing to share your feelings with me.
No, I don't. I still feel cheated by you. You were one way when we dated and then changed as soon as we were married.

I forgive you for withdrawing from me when I wanted to talk about our problems.
I am still angry about your silence.

I forgive you for not trying to make our marriage work.
Why couldn't you have tried more? We might have made it?

I forgive you for sitting around watching TV when I wanted to go out and have fun.
I still have a tough time understanding why you didn't want to be with me.

I forgive you for the times you said I was just like your mother.
I guess I may have acted the way she did at times. If you only had shared that with me earlier.

I forgive you for upsetting my life so much with this stupid divorce.
I have trouble forgiving you for this. I don't think it had to be this way.

After she identified these as her main hurts, she continued to write these "forgiveness statements" each day for a week until she had no more rebuttals or complaints. She began to feel the freedom that forgiving brings.

Another way is to take just one of the items you resent and write it again and again on the paper. List every rebuttal that comes to mind until you can say, "I forgive you for ___" several times without any objection arising in your mind.

✎ **Now do this activity. Use as many sheets of paper as you need.**

Most of us have better memories than God does. We cling to our hurts and nurse them. This causes us to have difficulty with others. We actually play God when we refuse to forgive others or ourselves. When we don't forgive, we not only fracture our relationship with others but with God as well. Do we help ourselves when we stick to a painful past? Do we help ourselves when we let the same old hurt wallop us again and again? Vengeance plants in your soul a videotape that you can't turn off. It plays the painful scene over and over inside your mind. It hooks you into its instant replays. Each time it replays, you feel the pain again. Does that help? Of course not.

When we don't forgive, we not only fracture our relationship with others but with God as well.

✎ **What painful scene plays over and over in your mind? Describe it below.**

_____

_____

Turn off the videotape

Forgiving means turning off that videotape. Doing this sets you free. Not forgiving inflicts inner torment on yourself. Forgiveness involves saying, "It is over. I no longer resent you or see you as an enemy. I love you, even if you cannot love me back."

Forgiving does not mean that what they did was OK or that they have permission to do it again. When we forgive, we perform spiritual surgery inside our souls; we cut away our own bitterness and anger over the wrong that someone did to us so that we can see our "enemies" differently. We detach that person from the hurt and choose to let it go. We count the debt paid. We know we have forgiven someone when in our hearts we begin to wish that person well. When we can pray for that person and ask for God's blessing on him or her, we have forgiven.

We can forgive because God has forgiven us (see Colossians 3:13 appearing at left.) Allowing God's forgiveness to permeate our lives and renew us is the first step toward wholeness.

To finalize your act of forgiveness, you can write a statement of release to the person who has hurt you. The woman we described earlier who struggled to forgive her ex-husband is a good example of what can happen in overcoming the hurt of the past. In her release statement she wrote:

> *Dear Jim,*
> *I release you from the responsibility I gave you to determine how I felt because of the divorce. I never understood all that happened to make you the way you were, and I probably never will. It doesn't matter now. What matters is that I release you from the bitterness and resentment I have held toward you during the past three years. I release you from my expectations of who and what you should have been. I forgive you.*

✎ **Stop and write your statement as this material suggests. Use a separate piece of paper for this exercise. Remember that this statement is for your eyes only; share it only with God; do not mail it.**

Pray for the strength of Jesus Christ in your life as you release your past to Him. Freeing that person through forgiveness gives you freedom as well. And in doing that, you can experience the abundance that Jesus Christ has for you.

❦ **Stop right now and pray for the strength of Jesus to forgive, as the paragraph you just read suggests.**

Pastor Dwight "Ike" Reighard had to deal with a special kind of pain in accepting the loss of his child who he never saw since both mother and infant died just before the baby's birth. Part of Reighard's "release" during this process was reading from 2 Samuel 12 which describes how David arose from his mourning after his son died, washed and anointed himself, changed his clothes, and went to the house of the Lord to worship. Reighard said David's words, "I shall go to him, but he shall not return to me" (2 Samuel 12:23) brought him encouragement.

The hope I have in Christ's promise of a happy eternity kept me sane.

Reighard said after the death of his wife Cindy and the baby: "I thought more about life after death than I ever had before. With all my heart I believe Cindy and my baby were escorted immediately by angels right into the presence of the Lord Jesus Christ. . . . The hope I have in Christ's promise of a happy eternity kept me sane in those grieving days."[2]

Another step in this process is desensitizing painful places and locations. Some people have changed jobs, avoided restaurants and favorite recreation-

Desensitizing painful places

al spots, and even changed churches because they were painful reminders of what used to be. But this is allowing the other person to control and dominate your life. You can choose to return to those places and take control of them. Perhaps you vacationed at some special places before your divorce, and you would like to return, but fear holds you back. Take a close friend or relative with you. Give this place to Jesus Christ in your prayers, and ask Him to take the pain away from that spot and to bless the location and the occasion. By returning, you dilute the pain.

✎ **In the margin write the name of one or two places you need to desensitize.**

Stage Five: Rebuilding and Stage Six: Resolution. At these stages, you finally can talk about the future with a sense of hope. You have just about completed your detachment from the other person. Hopefully you have done this without lingering fears. Healthy new attachments may occur at this time.

We can remember, however, that three possible outcomes exist for a relationship breakup: a change for the better; a change for the worse; or a return to the previous level of living. At the outset of the breakup, you hardly can conceive of things changing for the better, especially if you are the one who was rejected. In late stages of the crisis, you may see glimmers of possibility for positive change. Your judgments and decisions during this turning point in your life will make the difference in the outcome.

✎ **Write your memory verse in the margin three times from memory.**

❦ **Stop and pray, thanking God for helping you progress through the painful stages of recovery and on to rebuilding and resolution.**

Weekly Work

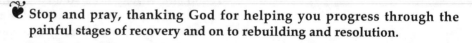 **Review this week's lessons. Pray and ask God to help you identify one positive statement that had an impact on your understanding of your loss. Write that statement in your own words.**

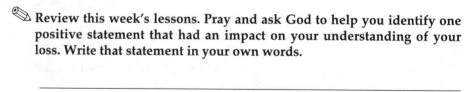

_____

Notes
[1]Gary Emery, Rh.D., *A New Beginning: How You Can Change Your Thoughts Through Cognitive Therapy* (New York: Simon & Schuster, Inc., 1981, 1988), 61.
[2]Dwight "Ike" Reighard, *Treasures from the Dark* (Nashville: Thomas Nelson, 1990), 163-164.

UNIT 9

Helping Others and Yourself

Case in point

TAKING THE LEAD

Shirley told her group: "I felt sad that my friend Charlotte has barely spoken to me since my father died. The two of us always confided in each other, but now she doesn't call me like she once did. Now I realize that Charlotte may feel uncomfortable being around me. She may fear that she'll fall apart when her own father, who is ill, dies.

"I see that I need to take the initiative to call her and tell her I understand why she's hesitant to be around me. It hurts a little to think that I have to call her, but if I help her in this way, it may free her to reach out to me."

Shirley was learning an important lesson about how to help friends and loved ones who may not be able to reach out to us in the way we desire when we're in a loss situation. In this unit you'll learn how to deal with these friends and loved ones, as well as how to help others who are grieving.

What you'll learn

This week you will
- identify four major "don'ts"—things that hurt rather than help grieving people;
- learn some positive ways to respond to people who hurt;
- discover how the Bible and others' words can help you minister to grieving people;
- describe some practical things you can do to help someone after a loss;
- determine how you can let loved ones know what they can do to help with your loss.

What you'll study

Hurting, Not Helping	Positive Ways to Respond	The Bible, Others Speak	Practical Things to Do	Helping Others Help You
DAY 1	DAY 2	DAY 3	DAY 4	DAY 5

Memory Verse

This week's verse of Scripture to memorize
Carry each other's burdens, and in this way you will fulfill the law of Christ.
–Galatians 6:2

Hurting, Not Helping

Today's Objective:
You will identify four major "do nots"—things that hurt rather than help grieving people.

Carry each other's burdens, and in this way you will fulfill the law of Christ.
–Galatians 6:2

"I would like to help. But I just don't know what to say. I'm sure I say too much, and sometimes I think what I say hurts more than it helps. So, most of the time, I stay away and don't do anything at all."

We all struggle with what to say, how to say it, and when to respond. Sometimes people don't know how to respond to us when we experience loss. In this unit, you'll learn how to help them know what to do and say.

As Christians, we can share Christ's love by the way we reach out to comfort and support others when they have endured a loss. (See this week's memory verse appearing at left.) We can follow certain guidelines in reacting to the grief of a friend or relative. We can choose to acknowledge the loss that has occurred and see it through the person's eyes rather than our own.

The Four Major "Do Nots"

In helping someone who sustained a loss, we can follow four major "do nots."
- Do not withdraw from the relative or friend.
- Do not compare, evaluate, or judge the person or his or her responses.
- Do not look for sympathy for yourself as you respond to the person.
- Do not pity the person.

In the case of any loss, a person needs continuing, ongoing support from several people—and not withdrawal. Sometimes the support we give is out of proportion. When a death occurs, people, calls, and cards often inundate the bereaved person. But two weeks later, the person feels like a social outcast. Nobody calls, nobody writes. The whole world seems to have gone merrily on its way, and the person feels alone. This creates a tremendous feeling of isolation. The bereaved person needs comfort on a consistent basis. He or she needs to be able to talk over what has occurred and to reminisce. In both death and divorce, major decisions need to be made. In all types of loss, people may need immediately a support group such as this one.

Avoid comparing

When you see your friend or relative, the most basic response is to ask how the person is doing and feeling. The important thing is to let the person talk without comparing, evaluating, or judging him or her. Here are some statements to avoid:

- "I don't understand why you're still crying. Life goes on, you know."
- "Look, you only lost your stepfather. What about your mother? She has a greater loss than you, and she's pulled herself together."
- "No one should feel that way about losing a cat. It's only an animal. You had it for 10 years, and you can find another one."
- "This will make your family closer. It's an opportunity to grow together."
- "I'm sure this will teach the other college students to be more diligent in their studies."
- "Don't you appreciate what you have left?"
- "You've started out in new jobs before, so just look at this layoff as a great opportunity—the way George did when he got fired."

Hurtful statements

Other statements that too many grievers have had to hear include:
- "Don't cry."
- "Be brave."
- "You'll get over it in a couple of weeks."
- "You shouldn't feel that way. After all, you have the Lord."
- "It's time to pull yourself together. You wouldn't want Mother seeing you that way, would you?"
- "We need to put the past behind us. Let's move on to the future with God."
- "At least he didn't suffer."
- "Well, just be glad it wasn't your only child."
- "Look at it this way—losing your husband this young and without children will make it easier for you to deal with."
- "Everyone dies sooner or later. He just died sooner."
- "The children need you to be strong."

Statements like this don't help or comfort. They only intensify the feelings of loss and despair.

✎ **Review the statements you just read. Put a check mark by those that others have said to you that you wished had never been said. Below add other statements like this that come to mind.**

_____

_____

The third "Do Not" involves seeking sympathy for yourself. Some people talk about their own sense of loss and grief in an effort to express sorrow and empathy. But you cannot expect the grieving person to help you at this time. This is the time for you to give, not receive. If you need assistance, get it from somebody else!

Feeling dependent

The fourth "Do Not" involves pity. If you pity someone, that person ends up feeling dependent and childlike. He or she begins to wallow in self-pity and to feel worse than before interacting with "helpful" you. Any kind of response or behavior which looks down on someone tends to reinforce the hurt and basically shows that you don't really care as much as you say.

✎ **Have you ever encountered the third or fourth "Do Not" as people have reacted to you in a loss situation? If so, below describe how you felt when that occurred.**

_____

_____

Put yourself in the other person's shoes as you approach someone after he or she has sustained a loss. Seek God's guidance to show you the most Christ-honoring way to respond.

❦ **Seek God's guidance now. Ask God to help you remember how sad or empty you felt when someone used one of the harmful approaches you just read about to try to help you. Ask Him to direct you to ways to help your loved one that will honor Christ and not hurt others.**

Begin to memorize Galatians 6:2, this week's Scripture memory verse. Below describe a time when you have carried someone else's burden, or when someone has helped you bear your burden.

_____

_____

DAY

2

Today's Objective:
You will learn some positive ways to respond to people who hurt.

Positive Ways to Respond

You can follow several positive guidelines in ministering to a friend, relative, or neighbor. The first step is simple. Accept what has happened and how the person is responding. You may have your own perspective on how he or she should be responding. Revise your expectations. You are not the other person or an authority on that individual's responses.

Accept grieving people and let them know their feelings are normal. Some of them will apologize to you for their tears, depression, or anger. You will hear comments like these: "I can't believe I'm still crying like this. I'm so sorry." "I don't know why I'm still so upset. It was unfair of them to let me go after 15 years at that job. I know I shouldn't be angry, but I guess I really am."

Facing feelings

You can be an encourager by accepting their feelings and the fact that they have feelings. Give them the gift of facing their feelings and expressing them. Here are some statements you can make to them:

- "I don't want you to worry about crying in front of me. Feeling this sad and not expressing it in tears is difficult. I may cry with you at times."
- "I hope you feel the freedom to express your sorrow in tears in front of me. I won't be embarrassed or upset. I just want to be here with you."
- "If I didn't see you cry, I would be more concerned. Your crying tells me you are dealing with this in a healthy way."
- "If I had experienced what you have been through, I would feel like letting the flood of tears come pouring out. Do you ever feel like that?"

 What have been the most helpful ways that people have responded to your tears? Check the statements above that apply, or below describe other helpful statements you've heard.

_____

_____

Anger is another feeling that many people have difficulty expressing. Use comments like these:
- "You are not being wrong or evil to feel angry about your wife's death. Your feelings demonstrate that you care. I feel angry too."
- "You are being honest with your feelings. Allow yourself to express your feelings, even if some people cannot understand or support you."
- "When you see other parents with healthy children, for you to feel angry and resentful over your son's illness is a normal response."

Your encouragement will help grieving people understand that their expression of feelings will not cause you to withdraw from them. Reassure them that you will not leave because of their feelings or that you will not try to talk them out of feeling the way they do.

Touch is another positive way of responding. Be sensitive to people who may not be as comfortable with touch as you are. If they seem to reject your physical gestures such as hugs or touch, respect them. Ask, "May I give you a hug?" If they seem hesitant, or if you extend a hand on the shoulder and they stiffen, this indicates that your brief words and physical presence will help more than touch will. In time, they may say to you, "I need a hug." Never assume that people don't need you. Find out by talking with them.

Another great gift you can give a hurting, grieving person is the gift of listening. When you listen to others, you give them a sense of importance, hope, and love that they may not receive any other way. Through listening, we nurture and validate the feelings of others.

Listening involves giving sharp attention to what someone else is sharing with you. Notice that I didn't say, "What someone is saying to you." Often what people share with us is more than what they say. We can listen to the total person, not just the words he or she speaks. Listening also means putting yourself in a position to respond to whatever the person is sharing with you.

Listening involves caring enough to take seriously what another person is communicating. When people know you hear them, they trust you and feel safe with you. If you are a good listener, others will be more likely to invite you into their lives. Those you listen to also may learn through your example to respond lovingly to what you share with them.

✎ **In the margin box list initials of people who model good listening skills for you.**

A difference exists between listening and hearing. Hearing involves gaining content or information for your own purposes. In hearing, you are concerned about what is going on inside you during the conversation. You are tuned in to your own reactions, responses, thoughts, and feelings.

Listening means caring for and empathizing with the person you listen to. You try to understand the speaker's thoughts and feelings. You listen for the person's sake, not your own. You don't think about what you will say when the speaker stops talking. You concentrate on what the person is saying.

In nurturing listening you listen for the emotional content behind the message the person shares. Then you reflect this back in an empathetic manner in your own words. Nurturing listening conveys support, caring, and acceptance for the person and his or her point of view.

✎ **Read the following dialogue in preparation to answer some questions about the conversation.**

Kathy: Hi, Anita. How are you?
Anita: Fine, I guess.
Kathy: I've wondered how you were getting along since your mother died.

People who are good listeners—

_____

_____

_____

_____

Ears that hear and eyes that see—the Lord has made them both.
–Proverbs 20:12

Anita: About as well as I can after losing Mom.

Kathy: I know it must have been tough for you. Losing a parent is a real loss.

Anita: I never realized how difficult it would be and that I'd still have sad times all these months later.

Kathy: When you have your parents in your life for so many years, you depend on their being there.

Anita: I know I should be able to put this behind me, but sometimes I just need to stop what I'm doing and reminisce and think about all the things we did together.

Kathy: It sounds like you have a lot of memories.

Anita: Would you think that I was crazy if I took off work on the one-year anniversary of her death and went back to the town where she grew up and visited some places that were important in her life?

✎ **After reading this dialogue, answer the following questions:**

1. Did Kathy give an opinion about what Anita should do? ❑ Yes ❑ No
2. Did Kathy advise Anita on a decision? ❑ Yes ❑ No
3. Did Kathy try to cheer up Anita? ❑ Yes ❑ No
4. Describe how Anita likely felt after the conversation with Kathy.

Retelling the details

_____

Kathy offered no opinions, gave no advice, and didn't try to cheer Anita. She simply listened reflectively in a way that nurtured Anita and made Anita feel understood. As you learn to nurture others with your listening, you can fill their need for understanding and acceptance.

Whether they have lost a pet, a job, a place, or a person, grieving people need to retell the details of their loss. They want to talk about the who, what, when, and how. Focusing on details and, in some cases, final conversations with someone they lost gives them a chance to hold on to whatever they lost. People will do this until they feel they will not lose the memory of the person they lost. When they reach that point, clinging to exact details will lessen.

When grieving people give the details, encourage them to tell about the accompanying feelings as well. They will feel relief as you listen without shock, embarrassment, or judgment. Above all, don't say too much to the hurting person. Let your presence do the talking rather than your words.

✎ **Below write one sentence about the details of your loss—the who, what, where, how. After you write it then write a sentence about how you felt about your loss.**

_____

_____

_____

Sydney answered this question this way: "My mother died of ovarian cancer on December 6, 1993, in a hospital in Ithaca, New York. I felt sad but also relieved because she suffered too long." The more we can focus on the feelings—and help others to do so—the more quickly healing begins.

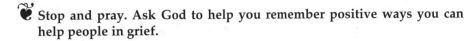 Stop and pray. Ask God to help you remember positive ways you can help people in grief.

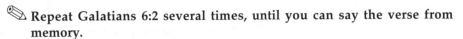 Repeat Galatians 6:2 several times, until you can say the verse from memory.

DAY 3

Today's Objective:
You will discover how the Bible and other's words can help you minister to grieving people.

The Bible, Others Speak

If you find yourself struggling with what to say, the written note or card is a wonderful way to comfort a griever. I have saved many of the written expressions we received after the loss of our son. They did two things for me: Those who wrote made me feel comforted and loved. Their expressions assisted me with my own expression of grief, because I felt the loss more sharply each time I read a note. You can send personal words of comfort, quotes, poems, and the Word of God. Scriptures such as the following are helpful:

The eternal God is your Refuge, And underneath are the everlasting arms.
–Deuteronomy 33:27, TLB

When you go through deep waters and great trouble, I will be with you. When you go through rivers of difficulty, you will not drown! When you walk through the fire of oppression, you will not be burned up—the flames will not consume you. For I am the Lord your God, your Savior, the Holy One of Israel …Don't be afraid, for I am with you.
–Isaiah 43:2, 3, 5, TLB

For I am persuaded, that neither death, nor life, nor angels, nor principalities, nor powers, nor things present, nor things to come, Nor height, nor depth, nor any other creature, shall be able to separate us from the love of God, which is in Christ Jesus our Lord.
–Romans 8: 38, 39, KJV

Even though I walk through the valley of the shadow of death, I fear no evil; for Thou art with me; Thy rod and Thy staff, they comfort me.
–Psalm 23: 4, NASB

God is our refuge and strength, a very present help in trouble.
–Psalm 46:1, KJV

He hath said, I will never leave thee, nor forsake thee.
–Hebrews 13:5, KJV

When I pray, you answer me, and encourage me by giving me the strength I need.
–Psalm 138:3, TLB

Be strong and of good courage, fear not . . . for the Lord thy God, he it is that doth go with thee; he will not fail thee, nor forsake thee.
–Deuteronomy 31:6, KJV

Trust in the Lord with all thine heart; and lean not unto thine own understanding. In all thy ways acknowledge him, and he shall direct thy paths.
—Proverbs 3:5, 6, KJV

✎ **What Scriptures have been most meaningful to you in your time of loss? Put a check mark by any of those just listed that apply, or below write one or two meaningful ones that were not in the list.**

_____

_____

_____

Appropriate poems are also available. Helen Steiner Rice has written many meaningful ones. You can find her books in most libraries and Christian book stores. Finding such comforting quotes takes a little extra time, but they may bring great healing in the life of someone who has suffered loss.

The prayers of others are helpful to share at the death of a loved one. The following is a prayer that can help a person face feelings:

I am empty, Father, I am bitter, even toward You. I grieve, not only for the one I have lost, but for the loving part of myself that seems to have died as well. You, who have at other times brought the dead back to life, revive my dead ability to live, to be close, to care about this world and those I know. I believe, I insist, that You can heal this mortal wound.[1]

One quality—patience—is highly necessary in ministering to a grieving person. You will hear the same story, the same details, the same tears again and again. This is necessary. What may be quite uncomfortable for you is anger. The extent of the person's anger may cause you to want to say, "Enough!" But anger is a healthy response if it is expressed within reasonable bounds.

You—the target

You even may become the target for the person's anger. If he or she withdraws, don't push the person. This is part of grief. The person may seem to move in and out of the real world and will progress at his or her pace, not yours. Try to avoid appearing irritated or impatient with the grieving one.

When the chance arises, you can bring up subjects that you and the grieving person have discussed before: the golf game, the favorite restaurant, trips you have taken, a hobby or craft. Ideally this encourages the grieving person to look forward by bringing some of the past into the future.

✎ **As you think about the grieving person you want to help, what subjects come to mind that you could use to help bridge the gap from past to future, as just described? Below, list them.**

_____

_____

_____

_____

Stop and pray. Ask God to direct you to Scriptures, writings of others, or other material that you can use to help people with their losses.

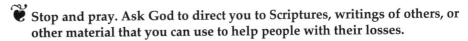 Work on this week's memory verse. Look back at page 113 if you need to refresh your memory. In the margin describe how listening to the details and helping the person face the future is part of carrying burdens.

DAY

4

Today's Objective:
You will describe some practical things you can do to help someone after a loss.

Practical Things to Do

You also can do many practical things to help, regardless of the type of loss. You can (1) discover the grieving person's personal situation and needs; (2) decide what you are willing and able to do for the person, realizing that you can't do it all, nor should you, and finally (3) contact the person and offer to do the most difficult of the jobs you have chosen. If the person rejects your offer, suggest another. Specific tasks could include delivering meals, yard work, making difficult phone calls, obtaining needed information about support groups or new employment, providing transportation, being available to run errands, and so forth.

You may need to help the grieving person accomplish several grief-work tasks. These tasks apply especially in the loss of a loved one and will be accomplished over a period of time.

1. Help grieving people identify secondary losses and resolve any unfinished business with the lost person. Many people never identify or grieve over these losses. Refresh your memory by rereading unit 2. Sometimes saying aloud what a grieving person never had an opportunity to say to the deceased helps complete some of the unfinished business.
2. Help them recognize that besides grieving for the lost person, they will need to grieve for any dreams, expectations, or fantasies they had for the person. This is sometimes difficult or overlooked.
3. Discover what the grieving people are capable of doing and where they might lack in their coping skills. Encourage positive things they are doing such as talking about the loss. When they do something unhealthy, such as avoiding reality, using alcohol, or excessive medication, help them identify other alternatives.
4. Provide them with helpful information about what they now are experiencing. Most people do not understand the duration and process of grieving. Don't let them equate the length and amount of grieving with how much they loved the person.
5. Let them know you understand they may want to avoid the intensity of the pain they presently experience. Encourage them to go through the pain of the grief. If they try to avoid it, it will explode at some other time.
6. Help them understand that their grief will affect all areas of life. It will affect work habits, memory, attention span, intensity of feelings, and response to a marital partner. This is normal.
7. Help them find ways to replenish themselves spiritually, socially, and physically. Be aware of their eating and exercise habits. Don't let them forego their own regular checkups.

Most people do not understand the duration and process of grieving.

8. Help them with the practical problems after a loss, and help in preventing unwise decisions. Such practical items as helping to arrange for meals, transportation, financial consultation, or eventually training or education needed for survival may be part of your task. Sometimes grieving people make major decisions too early. This creates additional losses. Some plan to sell their houses or move to new cities, but this may eliminate their roots or a needed support system. Discourage the person from making major changes during the first year if possible.

9. Help them reinvest in new lives. Some will need direction in getting back into the mainstream of life, especially if they cared for a chronically ill person for a period of time. Help them find support groups. Be especially careful of trying to promote too soon new dating activities for those who have lost spouses through death or divorce.

Here are some don'ts and do's:

Don'ts	Do's
Don't try to minimize their pain with comments like, "It's probably for the best," or "You're young; you can have another one."	Offer simple understanding statements such as, "I feel for you during this difficult time," or "I wish I could take the hurt away."
Don't just say, "Can I do anything to help?"	Offer specific things you can do. An example: "I'm on my way to the store. What can I pick up for you?" or "Would tomorrow be a good day to help with the laundry?"
Don't say "You shouldn't feel this way."	Encourage them to keep a journal or write down their thoughts and feelings.
Don't try to answer when they ask, "Why?" You don't have any answer, and at this time even the true answer may not be apparent.	Simply answer, "I don't know why. I guess both of us would like to have some answers at this time. I wish I had an answer to give you."
Don't offer spiritual answers as to why they face this problem. We don't know why tragedies happen and why certain people have to go through such trauma.	Give spiritual encouragement from your heart, and include Bible verses that have comforted you at difficult times. Let them know you will pray for them.
Don't ignore their needs after the immediate loss has subsided.	Keep in touch for months, especially at the critical times this book mentions.
Don't offer cliches or be vainly optimistic to cover up your insecurities.	Indicate your love by saying, "I feel really awkward because I'm not sure what to say, what you need, or how to help you, but I want you to know that I love you. I'm praying for you, and I'm available.[2]

✎ Add your own list to the don'ts and do's category, based on statements that have been helpful to you in your grief.

Don'ts	Do's
_____	_____
_____	_____
_____	_____

✎ Based on what you have just read, make a game plan for a grieving individual you may need to help. Below describe how you will accomplish some of the practical tasks this material has described

_____

_____

_____

_____

_____

❦ Stop and pray, asking God to help you do only the things that are helpful and not hurtful when you minister to grieving persons.

DAY 5

Today's Objective:
You will determine how to let loved ones know what they can do to help with your loss.

Helping Others Help You

Sometimes our friends and loved ones don't seem to know what to do to help us when we are grieving, so they are silent and do nothing. At other times their response comes straight off the "don't" list you just read. They make an effort to express their sympathy, and they bungle it badly. This leaves us feeling worse than before they spoke or acted at all.

You can take the lead and show them how you need them to help. You may think, "Me? Take the lead? Why should I have to do this, since I'm the one hurting?." You probably believe that having to set the pace for a friend or loved one is unfair. But you will do yourself and the other person a favor if you take the initiative to indicate what to do to help. That enables your friends to minister to you and gives them some guidelines for the next time they encounter someone in grief. Many people are capable of helping us carry our burdens if only we give them a gentle nudge. In unit 3 you learned a little bit about how to do this; we will expand on it here.

To begin with, be understanding. Keep your expectations low. Friends and loved ones can't understand your pain because they haven't had your experiences. Dwight "Ike" Reighard writes about this in _Treasures from the Dark:_ "You may find that grief is putting a strain on some of your relationships.

"No one really travels your road."

You need to be understood, and yet, it may be impossible for those who have not traveled the road to understand—and no one *really* travels *your* road. At a time when you are having to accept an unwanted loss, it is difficult to accept a friend or family member's lack of understanding. But it will lighten your own burden if you will lower your expectations of others, and accept their limitations, as well as their condolences."[3]

Secondly, try to think of specific things you do need, so that when someone asks the question, "What can I do to help?" you can give them some specifics. If you need someone to help write sympathy-acknowledgement cards, to accompany you to court as you probate a will, to help you sort through the deceased's belongings, to drive your child to a music lesson, to accompany you when you file for unemployment, or to simply sit with you while you talk about your loss and to pray with you, get your ideas ready. Most people who ask, "What can I do?" genuinely want some task to perform.

> ✎ **Practice doing this. Below jot down some specific needs you have that someone can help you do. Then, next time someone offers to help, reflect on the tasks you listed.**

How friends can help you

_____

_____

In unit 3 you received a photocopy of a letter that I suggested you send to family members, friends, acquaintances, or anyone who you feel should receive it. You can use this letter, or pen one in your own words, to state what life will be like for you, what they can expect from you, and what they can do for you. By doing this, you ease some of your pain by not having to repeat the same story over and over.

Here are some other suggestions about how you can help people help you. We adapt these from my wife's and my book, *I'll Love You Forever*, in which I write specifically about dealing with the loss of a dream for a child, but they can apply to any situation of loss:

- Touch carries a healing quality, as mentioned in an earlier day's study. Do not hesitate to ask for a hug from someone close to you when you need it.
- Ask people if they know others who have traveled this same path. Obtain their names, since they may be able to help you.
- Remember that when other people are uncomfortable with your situation, they are feeling, and by their nonverbal responses, saying, "I want you 'normal' as soon as possible, or at least I want you to act that way." No one should rob you of your feelings and your grief.
- Others may distance themselves from you because they don't want your discomfort invading their lives. You may feel they're afraid that what you've experienced may somehow be contagious. It may help to explain some of the adjustments you're experiencing. Tell people you understand how uncomfortable learning about your loss or life situation may be for them. Don't expect them to open up and say they're having difficulty with your situation. They probably won't admit it. But if you admit your struggle with your mixture of feelings, at least they may feel more comfortable.
- When you receive unsolicited advice, thank the people offering it for their concern and suggestions, and let them know they will add to the wealth

of information you've been gathering. You may want to work out a statement to use with well-meaning people. You could say, "I appreciate your concern and suggestions the other day. We've decided to follow this plan at this time. We've considered the various options, and we're comfortable with this for the time being. If it doesn't work, we're open to other possibilities."

- Friends may overwhelm you with help, to the point that they invade a family's boundaries and take away their decision-making opportunity. Determine how much assistance you want and establish boundaries with any intrusive friends or relatives.

Establish boundaries with intrusive friends or relatives.

When you take a positive, assertive step in reaching out to others and letting them know what you need, you'll gain confidence and strength. You'll feel less like a victim.[4]

✎ **Below describe what particular challenges you confront about how others are (or are not) helping you. Based on what you're read in this day's study, outline a game plan for dealing with these challenges.**

_____

_____

_____

_____

_____

One group member, Shirley, responded: "I felt sad that my friend Charlotte has barely spoken to me since my father died. The two of us always confided in each other, but now she doesn't call me like she once did. Now I realize that Charlotte may feel uncomfortable being around me because she worries she'll fall apart when her own father, who is ill, dies. I see that I need to take the initiative to call her and tell her I understand why she's hesitant to be around me. It hurts a little to think that I have to call her, but if I help her in this way, it may free her to reach out to me."

As you have walked through your own losses, you will be better able to help others walk through their valleys of loss. And you will learn to help them help you. The walk can be so lonely when it is undertaken alone. But when others come along to just be there, listen, weep, and comfort through their presence, grievers are sustained.

Jesus Christ is with us all of the time to encourage and support us.

None of us walks alone. Jesus Christ has been there, and He is with us all of the time to encourage and support us. Yes, life is full of losses, but Jesus Christ makes it possible to conquer them all.

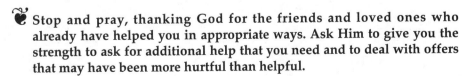 **Stop and pray, thanking God for the friends and loved ones who already have helped you in appropriate ways. Ask Him to give you the strength to ask for additional help that you need and to deal with offers that may have been more hurtful than helpful.**

✎ **Say this week's memory verse aloud three times.**

Weekly Work

 Review this week's lessons. Pray and ask God to help you identify one positive statement that had an impact on your understanding of your loss. Write that statement in your own words.

_____

_____

Congratulations! You have completed a very significant effort by working through this book. You probably do not feel that you have completed your grief process, and you will continue to grieve for a long while. You have, however, worked to equip yourself to grieve in ways that will lead to health, recovery, and discipleship. My prayer is that God will bless your grief process, that you will grow through your pain, and that you will experience an increased fellowship with God and usefulness as a fellow struggler in His kingdom.

_____

Notes

[1]Phyllis Hobe, *Coping* (Carmel, New York: Guideposts, 1983), 233.

[2]Lauren Briggs, *What You Can Say...When You Don't Know What to Say* (P.O. Box 8411, Redlands, California 92375), 150-155, adapted.

[3]Dwight "Ike" Reighard, *Treasures from the Dark* (Nashville: Thomas Nelson, 1990), 187.

[4]Norm and Joyce Wright, *I'll Love You Forever* (Colorado Springs: Focus on the Family Publishing, 1993), 151-154 (adapted).

Recommended Reading

Reading books by people who share ways they and others have coped with loss will enhance recovery. On these pages are some books that Christians frequently say helped them in their grief.

Alderman, Linda. *Why Did Daddy Die?* (New York: Pocket Books, 1989).

Billheimer, Paul. *Don't Waste Your Sorrows.* (Ft. Washington, PA: Christian Literature Crusade, 1977).

Cadmus, Ronald W. *God's Loving Embrace, A Touch that Comforts and Restores.* (Nashville: Thomas Nelson, 1990).

Carlson, Roberta. *Moments of Grace...Lessons from Grief.* (Wheaton, IL: Tyndale, 1987).

Chapin, Shelley. *Within the Shadow: A Biblical Look at Suffering, Death, and the Process of Grieving.* (Victor Books, 1991).

Comp, Diane, M.D. *A Window to Heaven.* (Grand Rapids, MI: Zondervan, 1992).

Cushenbery, Donald C. *Coping with Life After Your Mate Dies.* (Grand Rapids, MI: Baker Book House, 1991.)

Dunn, Ronald. *When Heaven Is Silent.* (Nashville: Thomas Nelson, 1984).

Fleece, Isabelle, and Bayley Joseph. *Not by Accident.* (Chicago: Moody Press, 1964).

Havner, Vance. *Though I Walk Through the Valley.* (Old Tappan, NJ: Revell, 1974).

Hayford, Jack. *I'll Hold You in Heaven: Healing and Hope for the Parent Who Has Lost a Child.* (Ventura, California: Regal, 1990).

Heavilin, Marilyn Willett. *Roses in December.* (San Bernardino, CA: Here's Life, 1986).

Holmes, Marjorie. *To Help You Through the Hurting.* (New York: Bantam, 1984).

Lewis, C.S. *A Grief Observed.* (New York: Bantam Books, 1961).

Malz, Betty. *Heaven: A Bright and Glorious Place.* (Old Tappan, NJ: Chosen Books, 1989).

Manning, Doug. *Don't Take My Grief Away.* (San Francisco: Harper & Row, 1984).

McGee, Robert S. *Search for Significance,* LIFE® Support Group Series Edition. (Houston: Rapha, 1992).

Price, Eugenia. *Getting Through the Night.* (New York: The Dial Press, 1982).

Reighard, Dwight "Ike." *Treasures from the Dark.* (Nashville: Thomas Nelson, 1990).

Richards, M. Gregory. *When Someone You Know Is Hurting: What You Can Do to Help.* (Grand Rapids, MI: Zondervan, 1994).

Sledge, Tim. *Making Peace with Your Past.* (Nashville: LifeWay Press, 1992).

Smith, Harold Ivan. *A Time for Healing: Coming to Terms with Your Divorce.* (Nashville: LifeWay Press, 1994).

continued on next page

Stanley, Charles. *Eternal Security: Can You Be Sure?* (Nashville: Thomas Nelson, 1990).

————. *How to Handle Adversity.* (Nashville: Thomas Nelson, 1989).

Stearns, Ann Kaiser. *Living Through Personal Crisis.* (Chicago: Thomas More Press, 1984).

Swindoll, Charles. *Growing Strong in the Seasons of Life.* (Portland: Multnoma Press, 1982).

Towns, James E. *Faith Stronger Than Death.* (Anderson, IN: Warner Press, 1975).

Wiersbe, Warren. *Why Us? When Bad Things Happen to God's People,* (Old Tappan, NJ: Fleming H. Revell Co., 1984)

Wright, Norm and Joyce. *I'll Love You Forever.* (Colorado Springs: Focus on the Family, 1994).

Yancey, Phillip. *Where Is God When It Hurts?* (Grand Rapids, MI: Zondervan, 1977).